Blazing Salads 2   Good Food Every Day

BLAZING SALADS 2

Good Food Every Day

LORRAINE FITZMAURICE

GILL & MACMILLAN

Gill & Macmillan
Hume Avenue
Park West
Dublin 12
with associated companies
throughout the world
www.gillmacmillanbooks.ie

© Lorraine Fitzmaurice 2013

978 07171 5056 4

Design by www.grahamthew.com
Photography by Joanne Murphy
Author photo by Mark Nixon, marknixon.com
Indexed by Cliff Murphy
Printed by Printer Trento, Srl, Italy

This book is typeset in 11 on 13pt Bembo.

The paper used in this book comes from the
wood pulp of managed forests. For every tree
felled, at least one tree is planted, thereby
renewing natural resources.

A CIP catalogue record for this book is
available from the British Library.

Acknowledgements

This book has come about with the hard work and dedication of Joe and Pamela in keeping the Blazing Salads deli a hub of good food and positive energy. Thanks for the consistent hard work and attention to detail from the Blazing Salads team.

A big thank you to Nora Mahony for bringing my thoughts and words together.

To my children, Pearl and Calum, for tasting all the recipes, and to Mark for becoming my agent.

I'd like to thank Pearl for all her help baking and cooking the many recipes for the photo shoot. You were fantastic.

To my mother, Pauline, for allowing me to take over her kitchen all those years ago, and then keeping my house in order while I focused on the cookbook.

Of course, none of this would have happened but for my father, Joe, introducing us to a healthy way of eating.

LORRAINE FITZMAURICE and her siblings had quite an unusual upbringing when it came to food. They were raised on macrobiotic cooking and their lunch boxes were the subject of much discussion in 1970s Irish classrooms. As revolutionary as it was at the time, this kind of cooking has become part and parcel of what it is to eat well today.

Lorraine and her siblings opened the Blazing Salads deli on Dublin's Drury Street in 2000, when she and her sister realised one lunch break that there was nowhere for vegetarians to get decent food. It continues to be a popular place among vegetarians and non-vegetarians alike.

Lorraine lives with her family in Clontarf, Dublin.

TABLE OF CONTENTS

MAIN DISHES ... 78

DESSERTS ... 150

Introduction

The first Blazing Salads cookbook was published in 2004. It was filled with recipes that had been created in the Blazing Salads restaurant and others that my siblings and I had enjoyed as children.

In 2000 we opened the Blazing Salads deli, which came about one day when my sister Pamela and I were sitting in St Stephen's Green in Dublin on our break from the restaurant. We realized that there was nowhere for vegetarians to get decent food on the go or to take back to the office. We decided Dublin needed a wholefood vegetarian deli. Our father, who is nothing if not a man of action, found a premises and rented it almost immediately, and we were away, running two family businesses at the same time. We're doing the same again these days, now with the bustling deli business and a wood-fired bakery run by my brother and sister-in-law, and we love the creative freedom that the more casual setting provides.

This new book, like the first, is made up of recipes to cook every day. Cooking daily is a joy because it's quick, easy, and has obvious benefits for your health and your wallet. What's more, cooking regularly at home will improve more than just family dinners – once you eat your last refrigerated triangle sandwich at your desk, you'll never look back. At its heart, our food is deli food; it's made to move and to be convenient, so you can have fresh salads that haven't been drowned in mayonnaise, protein-packed soups to keep you going, picnic and party food. There are plenty of vegan, gluten- and dairy-free options, and all of our recipes are versatile, so you can change them to suit your and your family's tastes, or to use what you have to hand.

We've gotten to know our customers over the years – and they're not quite who you might think. For one thing, many are meat-eaters. They're health- conscious, but not fanatical; they're eager to get more vegetables and 'good' fats into their diets, but just as interested in a slice of cake to round out their meal. Many work long hours and have learned that eating better in the middle of the day keeps you going for longer. They don't always have their cupboard stocked with wholefoods, but will pick out a few key ingredients to take home from the shop. But mostly, our customers are in it for the food. They want their food to be nutritious, of good quality, tasty and colourful, and like us, they're glad that the days of brown, heavy wholefoods are over.

Unlike most of our customers, it must be said that we had a pretty unusual upbringing when it came to food. My sister, two brothers and I were raised by very forward-thinking parents, and it didn't go unnoticed! My mother's macrobiotic cooking earned her the nickname of 'the witch' among the kids in the neighbourhood, and our lunch boxes were the subject of much discussion in 1970s Irish classrooms. As revolutionary as it was at the time, this kind of cooking has become part and parcel of what it is to eat well today, and little of it sounds so strange to us now. Its principles are simple: everything in moderation; take responsibility for your health; enjoy the best-quality ingredients that you can afford; and try to buy local.

Nothing connects you to your ingredients more than growing your own – and nothing, of course, is more local. Starting with a single flowerpot of your favourite herb on a sunny windowsill is easy, and that's just how I began growing my own, in a tiny apartment just off Patrick Street. Then, I moved up to a container garden in a small yard, and now, to a fully-fledged veg patch. Try growing your own vegetables. I started growing vegetables only in the last three years and have found it very satisfying. It's good fun, going out to the garden and digging up carrots or cutting Swiss chard and bringing it to the kitchen and cooking it straight away. When I was choosing the seeds with my father for this year's patch, I was already thinking about what recipes I was going to make. It's a fantastic way to get children of all ages interested in food, too: send them out to dig up the potatoes and they will start paying more attention to the whole cooking process. Next, move them on to doing small jobs for you in the kitchen, peeling and stirring, and in turn you can educate them on the importance of taking care with a knife or the heat from the cooker. When you all sit down for your meal, they will be interested in eating the dish and proud of having helped, and with luck, their love of food and cooking will take root and grow.

All of this can make food more enjoyable, but the greatest enjoyment is found in the cooking itself. I believe that energy plays a big part in food, and I like good energy in my food, from when the ingredients are grown, to the quality of the seasonings used, to the energy put in to the cooking of the food. To this end, it helps to start with a clear work surface and as clear a mind as you can muster. This can be a tall order in a hectic household, so if all else fails, turn the radio on to something you enjoy and focus on each task as you go, recentring yourself when you inevitably get interrupted. Because life is busy and making time to cook can be tricky, I like to cook simply, and without complication. These recipes are straightforward and easy to use: I only use one pot or one mixing bowl whenever I can, and as few steps and as little fuss as possible.

Cook well, eat well, and enjoy.

Lorraine Fitzmaurice

ZINGY RED SLAW, PAGE 19

Salads

Blazing Salads is more than just a play on a great film title:
our salads do something different.

Like everything we make at the deli, these salads are tasty,
wholesome, and good for you. They complement the other recipes
in this book, stand alone as meals, or both. They are light, bright and
packed with flavour, but they're even more important for
what they aren't.

Salads aren't diet food. They're not penitential. They're not limp,
swimming in mayonnaise, made of half-frozen iceberg lettuce or
spongy, pale tomatoes. They're not the garnish on the side of a
plate of 'real' food.

Our salads are real food.
Enjoy them with the best-quality ingredients.

CARROT AND DAIKON SALAD WITH FRESH CORIANDER

Daikon (also known as mouli) is a long white radish now grown locally in Ireland. Like the little round red radishes, it has a great peppery flavour, and helps the body flush out fat deposits. In Japanese cooking it is stirred into the soya sauce dip that comes with a deep-fried dish. It is also delicious steamed, very like our white turnips.

SERVES 4-6
2 CARROTS, ROUGHLY GRATED
DAIKON, HALF THE AMOUNT OF CARROT, ROUGHLY GRATED
SEA SALT
1 TBSP TOASTED SESAME OIL
$\frac{1}{2}$ TSP CUMIN SEEDS
$\frac{1}{2}$ TSP BROWN MUSTARD SEEDS
LEMON JUICE
2 TBSP FRESH CORIANDER (LEAVES AND STEMS)

1 Roughly grate the carrot and daikon into a large bowl. Add a pinch of sea salt. Heat the sesame oil in a pot, and when hot, add the cumin and mustard seeds. Allow to pop for about 30 seconds. Pour the popped seeds and hot oil over the carrot and daikon. Add a good squeeze of lemon juice, roughly chop the coriander and toss with salad. Season with sea salt and a little more lemon juice if needed.

TIP: Try replacing some of the grated carrot with grated raw beetroot. The earthiness of the beetroot works well with the cumin and the colour is fantastic.

AVOCADO SALADS

Avocados are packed with vitamins and essential 'good' fats. They're perfect for sandwiches and on veggie burgers, but here I've given a couple of favourite salads to show that you can do more with them than make guacamole.

To prepare the vegetables, peel, halve and remove the stones from the avocados and peel the cucumber, tomato and onion. Chop all of them into 2½ cm pieces and place in a large bowl.

TIP: To peel the tomatoes, remove the green top and cut a small x at the top of the tomato. Place in a bowl of boiling water for 2 minutes. Rinse under cold water and the skin should slip off easily. Cut the tomato in half and remove the seeds with your finger. Easy!

AVOCADO PICO DE GALLO SALAD

I was served this salad at a friend's house and just had to get (and share) the recipe. It is fiery with the jalapeño pepper, but it's balanced out by the fresh, zesty lime juice. See photo on page 5.

SERVES 6
3 AVOCADOS
1 RED PEPPER, DESEEDED
⅓ CUCUMBER
2 PLUM TOMATOES, PEELED AND DESEEDED
1 RED ONION, DICED
1 JALAPEÑO PEPPER, DESEEDED AND THINLY SLICED
1 TBSP FRESH CORIANDER
3 FRESH LIMES
1 TBSP EXTRA VIRGIN OLIVE OIL
SEA SALT

1 Roughly chop the fresh coriander, and add to the bowl of prepared vegetables, along with the jalapeño pepper. Season with sea salt and olive oil. Squeeze the limes and add the juice gradually to the salad until it tastes fresh and tart.

TIP: Before squeezing limes, roll them, hard, across a flat surface with the palm of your hand to soften the peel.

AVOCADO AND BLACK OLIVE SALAD

SERVES 6
3 AVOCADOS
⅓ CUCUMBER
1 RED ONION, DICED
3 PLUM TOMATOES, PEELED AND DESEEDED
25 G BLACK OLIVES, STONED
SEA SALT

FOR THE DRESSING:
1 TBSP EXTRA VIRGIN OLIVE OIL
2 TSP BROWN RICE VINEGAR
1 TBSP FRESH BASIL, FINELY CHOPPED
1 TBSP FRESH PARSLEY, FINELY CHOPPED
**2 TSP FRESH OREGANO, FINELY CHOPPED
(OPTIONAL)**

1 Roughly chop the olives and add to the bowl of prepared vegetables (see page 4).

2 Add all dressing ingredients to the salad and toss well. Season the vegetables with sea salt.

TIP: Brown rice vinegar has a lovely sweet/tart taste, but it can be replaced by red wine vinegar, which will be more tart.

SPELT PASTA SALAD WITH ROCKET

Many of our customers at the deli prefer to follow a wheat-free diet, but they still like to eat wholegrain foods. Wholemeal spelt pasta is lighter than wholewheat pasta, and it cooks faster, but feel free to use either.

SERVES 4 TO 6
125G WHOLEMEAL SPELT FUSILLI
125G WHOLEMEAL SPELT PENNE
40 G ROCKET
$^1/_2$ SMALL RAW BEETROOT
55 G PITTED BLACK OLIVES
2 SPRING ONIONS
1 TBSP FRESH PARSLEY, FINELY CHOPPED
SEA SALT

FOR THE DRESSING:
5 TBSP EXTRA VIRGIN OLIVE OIL
$2^1/_2$ TBSP RED WINE VINEGAR
1 SPRIG FRESH ROSEMARY, FINELY CHOPPED
SMALL PINCH DRIED CHILLI FLAKES (THEY'RE HOT!)
PINCH DRIED OREGANO
PINCH DRIED BASIL
PINCH SEA SALT

1 Cook the pasta in plenty of boiling salted water. NB: spelt pasta cooks very quickly. After 5 minutes, rinse in plenty of cold water. Drain well and place in a large bowl.

2 Rinse the rocket well and pick all the thick stalks from the leaves, keeping any stalks that are small and tender. Peel the beetroot and grate coarsely. Wash, trim and thinly slice the spring onion. Add the rocket, beetroot and spring onion to the pasta along with the pitted olives and parsley. Mix.

3 Whisk all the dressing ingredients together and dress and toss salad. Check the seasoning.

BEAN SALAD WITH BALSAMIC VINAIGRETTE

This is a full-flavoured and high-protein salad. Serve with a grain salad or some wholemeal or rye bread to make a complete protein and round out your meal.

SERVES 6 TO 8
350 G COOKED CHICKPEAS
350 G COOKED BLACK-EYED PEAS
350 G COOKED RED KIDNEY BEANS
175 G SWEETCORN
⅓ MEDIUM CUCUMBER
1 SMALL CARROT, ROUGHLY GRATED
3 SPRING ONIONS, FINELY SLICED
2 TSP FRESH PARSLEY, CHOPPED

FOR THE VINAIGRETTE:
3 TBSP OF EXTRA VIRGIN OLIVE OIL
3 TBSP OF BALSAMIC VINEGAR
1 LEMON
1 TSP DRIED ITALIAN HERBS, OR DRIED OREGANO OR BASIL
SEA SALT

1 Place the beans, peas and sweetcorn in a large mixing bowl.
2 Chop the cucumber, unpeeled, into small bite-sized pieces, and add to the bowl along with the grated carrot, spring onion and parsley.
3 Whisk all the dressing ingredients in a bowl, pour over the salad and mix well.
4 Place in the fridge to marinate for about 30 minutes before serving.

TIP: Remember, you don't have to stick to the beans listed above for this salad – use whatever beans you like, and whatever you have to hand. It's a great way to make a quick and easy new meal with any left over beans, and it works particularly well with green, brown and puy lentils as they soak up the flavours of the dressing if left for a short time before serving.

CHICKPEA SALADS

Chickpeas are an absolute storecupboard staple. They're very cheap, available everywhere, and take on the biggest flavours you can throw at them. Buying organic chickpeas, beans and pulses only costs a few cent more for a serious difference in quality.

I like to use dried chickpeas, and soak mine overnight, or in the morning for cooking after work, but tinned are fine, and are ready in an instant.

CHICKPEA, RED ONION AND CHILLI SALAD

SERVES 4 TO 6
225 G COOKED CHICKPEAS
1 SMALL RED ONION, THINLY SLICED
1 SMALL COOKED, DICED CARROT
2 LEAVES COS LETTUCE, FINELY SLICED
3 TBSP EXTRA VIRGIN OLIVE OIL

1 TSP FRESH CHILLI, DESEEDED AND MINCED
3 TBSP LEMON JUICE
1 TSP GARLIC, MINCED
1 HEAPED TBSP FRESH PARSLEY, FINELY CHOPPED
SEA SALT

1 Place the olive oil, lemon juice, chilli and garlic in a pot. Bring to a boil, remove from the heat and set aside.

2 Place the chickpeas, red onion, carrot, lettuce and parsley into a large bowl. Season with a little salt. Mix. Pour the warmed dressing over the salad vegetables and mix well. Check the seasoning.

TIP: This salad works well with either green or puy lentils instead of the chickpeas.

CHICKPEA SALAD WITH TAHINI AND MUSTARD DRESSING

SERVES 4 TO 6
225 G COOKED CHICKPEAS
1 SMALL COOKED CARROT, DICED
1/4 CUCUMBER, DICED
1 TOMATO, DICED
1/2 SMALL RED ONION, DICED
1 TBSP CHOPPED FRESH PARSLEY

FOR THE DRESSING:
5 TBSP OF LIGHT TAHINI
2 TBSP LEMON JUICE
1 TBSP DIJON MUSTARD
PINCH OF SEA SALT

1 Whisk the dressing ingredients in a bowl. Add 2 or 3 tbsp water and blend until smooth and creamy.

2 In a separate bowl place the chickpeas, vegetables and parsley. Pour the dressing over the vegetables and mix well. Season.

TIP: The dressing for this salad will keep refrigerated for 3 weeks. It is also a good alternative to mayonnaise in coleslaw.

SPICY NOODLE SALAD

Moong (or mung) noodles are also known as thread or glass noodles and are used in Asian cooking. They are made from nothing but moong beans, and are gluten- and fat-free. Moong noodles are common in stir-fries, and can be stirred into soups for extra texture, but I think they are the perfect noodle for salads, as they cook in just five minutes and soak up tasty dressings.

SERVES 4 TO 6
55 G RAW MOONG NOODLES
25 G WHITE CABBAGE
1 SMALL CARROT
1/4 RED PEPPER
1/4 YELLOW PEPPER
1 TBSP ROASTED RED SKINNED PEANUTS, ROUGHLY CHOPPED
1 TSP FRESH CORIANDER
1/2 RED CHILLI, DESEEDED AND MINCED
1 TSP SPRING ONION, FINELY SLICED
1 TSP FRESH PARSLEY, FINELY CHOPPED
1 TBSP TOASTED SESAME OIL
1 TSP BALSAMIC VINEGAR
2 TSP SOYA SAUCE

1 Place the noodles in a pot with plenty of boiling water for 5 minutes. Rinse in cold water. Drain well and roughly chop and place in a large bowl. Finely shred the white cabbage, roughly grate the carrot and slice the peppers into fine 2½ cm slices. Add all vegetables to the noodles, along with the peanuts, chopped coriander, chilli, spring onion and parsley. Toss well. Whisk the toasted sesame oil, soya sauce and balsamic vinegar together and add to the vegetables and noodles. Mix well. Check the seasoning and adjust the flavour using the balsamic vinegar and soya sauce.

TIP: Try this salad warm on a chilly day. Place on a hot pan and toss until heated through.

TIP: Add deep-fried tofu (p. 141) for extra protein.

TIP: Any fine noodle can be used in this salad: angel hair, egg or soba or rice noodles all work well, as long as they are fine.

POTATO SALADS

Potato salad can be prepared in advance, so it's ready to go to accompany a quick meal, and the varieties with beans make for a good lunch. If you already have leftover cooked potatoes, this is a great way to use them up.

These light, tasty and wholesome salads will put the mushy, mayonaissey monstrosities of your newsagent's deli counter to shame.

To prepare the potaoes, pick firm, new potatoes, and boil in lightly salted water until just cooked but not mushy. Slice thickly or quarter, place in a large bowl and set aside to cool. Season with a pinch of salt.

NEW POTATOES WITH PINTO BEANS, RADICCHIO AND BALSAMIC

This recipe was given to the deli by our Croatian chef Sasa some time back and remains a favourite.

The richness of the balsamic vinegar and the sharpness of the radicchio balance out the potatoes – gorgeous-looking salad with all its striking shades of red.

SERVES 4-6
250 G NEW POTATOES
100 G PINTO BEANS, COOKED
40 G RADICCHIO, FINELY SLICED
25 G RED ONION, DICED
1 HEAPED TBSP CHOPPED FRESH PARSLEY
1¹/₂ TBSP EXTRA VIRGIN OLIVE OIL
1¹/₂ TBSP BALSAMIC VINEGAR
SEA SALT

1 Place the prepared potatoes in a large bowl and set aside to cool slightly. Add the beans, radicchio, red onion and parsley to the halved potatoes. Season with salt. Pour over the olive oil and balsamic vinegar and mix well. Check the seasoning, and serve.

TIP: Red kidney beans or black-eyed peas also work well.

NEW POTATOES WITH MOONG BEANS AND FRESH DILL

Light, fresh dill just works with potatoes, and the gherkins add a good tanginess.

SERVES 4 TO 6
250 G NEW POTATOES
100 G MOONG BEANS, COOKED, RINSED AND
  DRAINED
40 G CUCUMBER, PEELED AND DICED
PICKLED GHERKIN, 2½ CM PIECE
  OR 2 COCKTAIL GHERKINS

2 TSP FRESH DILL, FINELY CHOPPED
2 TSP FRESH PARSLEY, FINELY CHOPPED
1 TBSP EXTRA VIRGIN OLIVE OIL
1 TSP RED WINE VINEGAR
SEA SALT

1 Add the moong beans to the cooled prepared potatoes along with the chopped cucumber. Wash the gherkin to remove some of the tart flavour and mince. Add to the potatoes along with the fresh dill and parley. Mix the olive oil and red wine vinegar together and add to the salad. Toss all the ingredients together well. Season to taste.

NEW POTATOES WITH SWEETCORN AND CELERY

SERVES 4 TO 6
250 G NEW POTATOES
SEA SALT
85 G SWEETCORN
1 STICK CELERY, SLICED
1 TBSP RED ONION, DICED
1 CLOVE GARLIC, MINCED
1 TBSP FRESH CORIANDER, FINELY CHOPPED
EXTRA VIRGIN OLIVE OIL
RED WINE VINEGAR

1 Once the prepared potatoes are cool, add the sweetcorn, celery, red onion, garlic and coriander. Mix. Whisk 3 tbsp olive oil and 1½ tbsp red wine vinegar together and pour over the salad. Mix well and check the seasoning.

RICE SALAD WITH ROASTED ROOT VEGETABLES

SERVES 6

250 G ORGANIC SHORT GRAIN BROWN RICE
SEA SALT
1 CARROT, DICED INTO 1 CM CUBES
DAIKON, SAME AMOUNT AS CARROT, DICED INTO 1 CM CUBES
1 SMALL ONION, DICED INTO 1 CM CUBES
UNREFINED SESAME OIL
SUNFLOWER OIL FOR DEEP FRYING
1/2 CUBE TOFU, DICED INTO 1 CM CUBES
SOY SAUCE
1/2 SHEET NORI SEAWEED, THINLY SLICED
FRESH GINGER
FRESH PARSLEY
25 G TOASTED PUMPKIN, SUNFLOWER OR SESAME SEEDS

1 Preheat the oven to Gas 7/220°C/425°F.

2 Rinse the rice and place in a heavy-bottomed pot. Add 450ml water and a small pinch of salt. Bring to a boil, lower the heat, cover tightly and simmer for 1 hour. Stir, place in a large bowl and set aside to cool.

3 Place the carrot, daikon and onion in an ovenproof dish. Season with a little salt and toss with 1 tbsp sesame oil. Place on the top shelf of the preheated oven and roast for 20 minutes until the vegetables are cooked. Stir once during roasting. Set aside to cool.

4 Heat the sunflower oil for deep-frying, and fry the tofu (see page 141 for the how-to). Drain on a piece of paper towel. Toss in some soya sauce to taste. Add the roasted vegetables, tofu and nori to the cooked rice. Toss well.

5 Pour 2 tbsp soya sauce into a small bowl. Finely grate 1 tsp fresh ginger, gather the pulp in the palm of your hand and squeeze some drops into the soya sauce, about ½ tsp. Gradually season the rice salad to taste with the soya sauce and ginger mixture. Stir in 2 tsp finely chopped fresh parsley. Place in a serving bowl and scatter with toasted pumpkin seeds.

TIP: This salad is lovely – and quicker – using barley instead of rice; barley needs only 45 minutes' simmering time.

BULGUR SALAD WITH BUTTERNUT SQUASH AND ADUKI BEANS

SERVES 4 TO 6
315 G COARSE WHOLEMEAL BULGUR WHEAT
SEA SALT
2¹/₂ TBSP EXTRA VIRGIN OLIVE OIL
3¹/₂ TBSP LEMON JUICE
1 FRESH CHILLI, DESEEDED AND MINCED
2 TBSP FRESH CORIANDER
2¹/₂ TBSP FRESH MINT
150 G DICED ROASTED BUTTERNUT SQUASH
100 G COOKED ADUKI BEANS
1 CM PIECE OF KOMBU SEAWEED (OPTIONAL)

1 Rinse the bulgur, place in a large bowl and just cover with cold water. Soak overnight, or in the morning to use that night. Fluff up the soaked bulgur. Season with sea salt. Add olive oil and lemon juice. Stir well. Check the seasoning. Wash the coriander, and chop both leaves and stems very finely. Remove the hard stalks from the mint, rinse and chop very fine along with the mint leaves. Add the herbs to the bulgur along with the chilli, butternut squash and aduki beans. Mix well.

2 Aduki beans are available cooked in tins in health food stores, but this is how to cook the beans yourself: Place the aduki beans in a bowl and wash well. Cut a 1 cm piece of kombu seaweed (if using) and wipe the salt from it. Place in the bowl with the aduki beans. Cover with plenty of cold water. Soak overnight or for 6–8 hours. Drain off the soaking water and place the beans and seaweed in a pot with 250 ml water. Cover and bring to a boil. Lower the heat and simmer for 45 minutes. Rinse and drain to use in salad. If using in a casserole or soup, there's no need to rinse after cooking.

3 To roast butternut squash, heat the oven to Gas 7/220°C/425°F. Peel 1 small butternut squash and remove the seeds. Chop into 1 cm cubes and place on a baking tray. Season with a small pinch of salt and add 1 tbsp extra virgin olive oil. Toss well. Place on the top shelf of the preheated oven for 20 minutes until the squash is tender but not mushy.

TIP: This salad is equally good made with wholemeal couscous or quinoa.

SLAW

Like potato salad, coleslaw is usually a sad sight, drenched in mayonnaise. These crunchy, refreshing salads celebrate good produce with healthy dressings, and make a great addition to any summer meal.

To shred your cabbage, turn it on its side and hold the bottom end. Using a large, sharp knife, slice as thinly as you can from the top. When you get towards the middle, cut out the heart and the stem you were holding and discard, shredding the rest of the leaves as finely as you can and place in a large bowl.

WHITE CABBAGE SALAD WITH DULSE

Don't let the seaweed put you off this fresh, delicious salad! See photos, page 20.

SERVES 4 TO 6
25 G DULSE SEAWEED
280 G WHITE CABBAGE, SHREDDED
2 LEAVES COS LETTUCE, SHREDDED
1 MEDIUM CARROT, ROUGHLY GRATED
1 TSP FRESH PARSLEY, FINELY CHOPPED
2 TBSP EXTRA VIRGIN OLIVE OIL
2 TSP RED WINE VINEGAR
1/2 TSP DRIED OREGANO
SEA SALT
COARSELY GROUND BLACK PEPPER

1 Rinse the dulse well. Place in a small bowl and cover with 3 tbsp water. Set aside to soak for 20 minutes.

2 Finely slice the lettuce and add to your prepared cabbage. Coarsely grate the carrot and add to the bowl along with the parsley. Drain the seaweed and roughly chop and add to the salad.

3 Place the olive oil, red wine vinegar, dried oregano, a pinch of salt and pepper into a bowl and whisk. Pour over the salad and mix well.

4 Make the salad at least 30 minutes before serving to allow the flavours to develop. Check the seasoning and adjust accordingly using the red wine vinegar and sea salt.

ZINGY RED SLAW

Hands down my favourite salad at the deli, this is perfect for a barbeque. It's just as bright and refreshing to eat as it looks (see photo, page xvi).

SERVES 4 TO 6
175 G RED CABBAGE, SHREDDED
175 G WHITE CABBAGE, SHREDDED
1 MEDIUM CARROT, ROUGHLY GRATED
2 TBSP SPRING ONION
20 G TOASTED SEEDS (PUMPKIN, SESAME, SUNFLOWER)

FOR THE DRESSING:
3 TBSP SUNFLOWER OIL
3 TBSP RICE VINEGAR
2 TSP AGAVE SYRUP OR CLEAR HONEY
1/2 TSP GRATED FRESH GINGER
1 TBSP FRESH CORIANDER, CHOPPED FINELY
SMALL PINCH CHILLI FLAKES
PINCH SEA SALT

1 Place all the vegetables and seeds in a large bowl and toss together. In a small bowl whisk all the dressing ingredients together. Pour over the vegetables and toss well.

2 This salad will keep well in the fridge for 4 or 5 days.

3 To toast the seeds, toss together on a dry pan over a medium heat for 3–4 minutes, taking care not to scorch them.

TIP: To enjoy the toasted seeds as a snack, toss them in soy sauce while warm.

WHITE CABBAGE SALAD WITH DULSE, PAGE 18

QUINOA

Quinoa is full of protein, which makes these salads excellent lunches.

QUINOA WITH ROASTED RATATOUILLE VEGETABLES AND FRESH BASIL

See photo overleaf.

SERVES 4 TO 6
1 RED ONION, CUT INTO 1¹/₂ CM DICE
1 AUBERGINE, CUT INTO 1¹/₂ CM DICE
1 COURGETTE, CUT INTO 1¹/₂ CM DICE
1 RED PEPPER, CUT INTO 1¹/₂ CM DICE
2 CLOVES GARLIC, ROUGHLY CHOPPED
DRIED BASIL
SEA SALT
EXTRA VIRGIN OLIVE OIL
1 400 G TIN CHOPPED TOMATOES
COOKED QUINOA (SEE PAGE 129)
2 TBSP FRESH PARSLEY
1 TBSP FRESH BASIL
25 G TOASTED PINE NUTS (OPTIONAL)

1 Preheat the oven to Gas 7/220°C/425°F.

2 Place the red onion, aubergine, courgette, red pepper and garlic in an ovenproof dish. Add the garlic, 2 tbsp olive oil, and a good pinch each of dried basil and sea salt. Toss well to coat all the vegetables. Place on the top shelf of the preheated oven for 10 minutes. Remove from the oven and stir in the tomatoes. Return to the oven for a further 15 minutes until the vegetables are soft.

3 Fluff up the cooked quinoa, place in a large bowl and set aside to cool.

4 Season the quinoa with sea salt. Add 1 tbsp olive oil, chopped fresh parsley and chopped fresh basil. Mix well. When the roasted vegetables have cooled, stir into the quinoa salad. Season. Serve scattered with toasted pine nuts.

TIP: Serve with crumbled feta cheese.

TIP: This salad works well using bulgur or wholemeal couscous instead of the quinoa.

QUINOA TABOULLEH

SERVES 4 TO 6
COOKED QUINOA (SEE PAGE 129)
1 TBSP EXTRA VIRGIN OLIVE OIL
1 TBSP LEMON JUICE
SEA SALT
1 TBSP FRESH MINT, CHOPPED
2 TBSP FRESH PARSLEY, CHOPPED
1 TOMATO, DICED
¼ CUCUMBER, DICED

1 Fluff up the cooked quinoa, place in a large bowl and set aside to cool.

2 Remove the hard stalks from the mint and chop very finely along with the parsley.

3 Season the quinoa with sea salt, olive oil and lemon juice to taste. When a well-rounded, balanced flavour is reached, add the chopped mint and parsley. Mix well. Stir in the tomato and cucumber. Check the seasoning one last time. Serve.

TIP: It helps to be generous with the olive oil and lemon juice in this recipe.

QUINOA WITH ROASTED RATATOUILLE VEGETABLES AND FRESH BASIL, PAGE 22

BARLEY AND LENTIL SALAD WITH RADISH AND NORI

I like to add a seaweed to grain salads because, along with some fresh veg, it makes for a nutritionally complete meal. Nori holds up well in a salad, and the shiny black colour looks stunning with the red circles of radish, and the green onion and parsley.

SERVES 4 TO 6
225 G BARLEY
15 G NORI SEAWEED, ABOUT ³/₄ SHEET
SOYA SAUCE
6 RED RADISHES
2 SPRING ONIONS
100 G GREEN OR PUY LENTILS, COOKED
1 TBSP FRESH PARSLEY, FINELY CHOPPED
1 TBSP EXTRA VIRGIN OLIVE OIL
2 TBSP LEMON JUICE
1 TBSP WHOLEGRAIN MUSTARD
SEA SALT

1 Rinse the barley well. Place in a pot with 750 ml water and a pinch of salt. Bring to a boil, cover, lower the heat and simmer for 30 minutes. When the barley is cooked, rinse in plenty of cold water to remove the starch. Drain well and set aside.

2 Cut the sheet of nori into three strips, and slice the strips into thin pieces. Add to the barley. Wash, top and tail the radishes and slice thinly. Add to the bowl. Wash and trim the spring onion. Thinly slice both white and green parts and add to the bowl along with the lentils and parsley. Mix.

3 Whisk together the olive oil, lemon juice, wholegrain mustard and a pinch of salt. Pour over the barley and vegetables and mix well. Check the seasoning.

TIP: This is a great lunchbox salad. It has everything you need for an energy boost from protein, amino acids and minerals and is vitamin rich.

Savouries

I find that cooking, all cooking, is fun, but then again, I suppose I would. If you're looking for inspiration, then this is for you.

This is fun food to share, to serve with drinks and to pass around at parties. It's what you'll get asked to do for birthday dinners and bring to barbecues, and the sort of dish people want the recipe for. These burgers, turnovers and small bites always go down a treat, thanks as much to the atmosphere they help to create as for the food itself.

FALAFEL WITH TAHINI AND LEMON DRESSING

Falafel is a great form of protein, popular as a snack and sandwich filling across the Middle East. In pitta bread with a bit of salad it's a sandwich, on toothpicks it's a canapé, and with a plate full of roasted aubergine (p. 148), halloumi (p. 135) or stuffed tomatoes (p. 107), it's part of a bountiful buffet dinner.

MAKES 16 PATTIES
315 G CHICKPEAS
1/2 MEDIUM RED ONION, DICED
1 TBSP FRESH MINT
1 1/2 TBSP FRESH CORIANDER
1 CLOVE GARLIC

SEA SALT
2 TSP LEMON JUICE
SUNFLOWER, PEANUT OR SOYA OIL FOR DEEP FRYING
PITTA BREAD, TO SERVE
ALFALFA OR BEAN SPROUTS, TO SERVE

1 Rinse the chickpeas. Place in a bowl and cover with water and soak for at least 6 hours or overnight. Remove any hard stalks from the mint. Rinse the mint leaves and the coriander leaves and stalks.

2 When the chickpeas have soaked, blend the chickpeas with a food processor for a minute. They're still raw at this stage, but the best falafel is made with raw chickpeas, as they hold their shape better and retain more of their flavour. Turn off the motor and add the mint, coriander, garlic, lemon juice and a pinch of sea salt. Blend until all the ingredients are well mixed. Empty the blended mixture into a bowl and season with sea salt and lemon juice to taste.

3 Heat the oil for deep-frying. To check that the oil is hot enough, drop a small piece of bread into the oil; it should drop to the bottom and pop back up to the top immediately, sizzling furiously.

4 Weigh the mix into 25 g portions. With slightly dampened hands, shape the portions into patties about 1cm thick. Alternately, wet two dessertspoons and scoop up a dessertspoonful of falafel mix, using the other spoon shape the patty. Drop into the hot oil.

Fry 5 or 6 falafel at a time for 2–3 minutes to cook. Drain on kitchen paper.

TO MAKE A TAHINI AND LEMON DRESSING:
3 TBSP LIGHT TAHINI   **SEA SALT**
1 TBSP LEMON JUICE

1 Place the tahini and lemon juice in a bowl. Add a pinch of salt. Whisk in enough water to make a smooth creamy dressing, approx. 3 tbsp. Season with sea salt and lemon juice to taste.

2 Toast the pitta bread and slice open one end. Fill with salad vegetables and falafel balls and drizzle with the tahini dressing. Top with alfalfa or bean sprouts to add extra crunch.

3 Falafel can also be eaten as finger-food with the tahini and lemon dressing or yoghurt and mint dressing (p. 109) as a dip.

TIP: Falafel will keep for 4–5 days in the fridge and can be eaten cold or heated in a moderate oven.

TURNOVERS

Turnovers appear around the world in many guises – think Cornish pasties, empanadas from Central America, or Indian samosas – but the basic recipe is homemade dough stuffed with what you fancy, then fried or baked. They're portable in either a larger size for lunch, or smaller, for party food. We use spelt wholemeal flour for our pastry because our customers want a wheat-free alternative, but we discovered that it's also easier to work with, as it's less sticky. Any wholemeal flour can be used in the pastry for a nutty, deep flavour.

The first two recipes use pizza dough (p. 52), and are baked in the oven. To shape the turnovers, dust 2 baking trays with wholemeal flour. Divide the dough into twelve 50 g balls of dough. On a floured surface, knead each ball of dough for a few seconds. Using a rolling pin, roll the dough into a 12 cm circle. Spoon a tablespoon of your filling mix onto the circle. Fold the dough over the vegetables to form a crescent shape, and press a floured fork along the edges of the dough to seal the turnover. Continue until all the turnovers are made. Place on the floured baking trays in the preheated oven for 25–30 minutes until the pastry begins to brown.

BUTTERNUT SQUASH AND SWEET POTATO TURNOVERS

MAKES 20
PIZZA DOUGH (SEE PAGE 52)

500 G BUTTERNUT SQUASH
400 G SWEET POTATO
EXTRA VIRGIN OLIVE OIL
SEA SALT
2 TSP CUMIN SEEDS
2 TSP BROWN MUSTARD SEEDS
1 ONION, DICED
1 CHILLI, DESEEDED AND MINCED
400 G TIN TOMATOES, CHOPPED
2 TBSP TOMATO PURÉE
100 G SWEETCORN
200 G ADUKI BEANS, COOKED
1 TBSP PARSLEY, CHOPPED

1 Preheat oven to Gas 7/220°C/425°F. Peel, deseed and chop the butternut squash and peel and chop the sweet potato into 1 cm pieces. Place on a baking tray or in a roasting tin and add a good pinch of sea salt and 3 tbsp olive oil. Toss well. Place on the top shelf of the preheated oven and roast for 30 minutes until the vegetables are soft but not mushy. Set aside to cool.

2 Lower oven temperature to Gas 4/180°C/350°F.

3 Heat 1 tbsp olive oil in a pot. Add the cumin and mustard seeds and allow to pop for 1 minute. Add the onion and chilli and cook over a medium heat until the onion is soft but not browned. Add to the roasted butternut squash and sweet potato, along with the chopped tinned tomatoes and the tomato puree. Stir in the sweetcorn, cooked aduki beans and parsley. Check the seasoning, and set aside.

TIP: These turnovers will keep well refrigerated for 1 week. Once cool, they will also freeze well in freezer bags for up to 3 months.

MEDITERRANEAN VEGETABLE AND FETA TURNOVERS

MAKES 12
PIZZA DOUGH (SEE PAGE 52)

1 LARGE RED ONION
1 RED PEPPER
½ AUBERGINE
½ COURGETTE
2 CLOVES OF GARLIC, MINCED
1 TSP DRIED ITALIAN HERBS, OR OREGANO, BASIL OR MIXED HERBS
SEA SALT
EXTRA VIRGIN OLIVE OIL
400 G TIN TOMATOES, CHOPPED
1 TBSP FRESH BASIL, CHOPPED
150 G FETA CHEESE

1 Preheat oven to Gas 7/220°C/425°F. Chop the red onion, red pepper, aubergine, courgette into 1 cm cubes. Place on a baking tray or roasting tin. Add the garlic, dried herbs, a good pinch of sea salt and 4 tbsp olive oil. Toss well together. Place on the top shelf of a preheated oven. Roast for 15 minutes. Remove the vegetables from the oven and stir in the chopped tomatoes. Return to the top shelf of the oven and roast for a further 30 minutes. Check the season. Set aside to cool.

2 Lower oven temperature to Gas 4/180°C/350°F.

3 Stir the basil and crumbled feta cheese into the cooled roasted Mediterranean vegetables. Check the seasoning.

4 Fill, shape and bake dough as instructed above.

TIP: These turnovers will keep well refrigerated for 1 week. Once cool, they will also freeze well in freezer bags for up to 3 months.

ARAME TURNOVERS WITH CARROT, GINGER AND SESAME

I have fond memories of my mother making these turnovers for us when I was younger.

MAKES 12

FOR THE WHOLEMEAL PASTRY DOUGH:
300 G WHOLEMEAL SPELT PASTRY
150 G SUNFLOWER MARGARINE
SEA SALT

FOR THE FILLING:
UNREFINED SUNFLOWER OIL
1 SMALL CARROT, JULIENNED
3 SPRING ONIONS, SLICED IN ROUNDS
300 G ARAME SEAWEED, COOKED
SOYA SAUCE
1 TSP FRESH GINGER, FINELY GRATED
SESAME OR SUNFLOWER SEEDS
SUNFLOWER, PEANUT OR SOYA OIL FOR DEEP-FRYING

1 To make the pastry, place the flour in a large bowl, add a pinch of sea salt, and rub in the margarine until the mix resembles breadcrumbs. Add 60–80 ml water gradually and with your fingertips bring it together until a ball of dough forms. Wrap the dough in cling film and place it in the fridge to rest for at least 30 minutes.

2 Heat 2 tbsp sunflower oil in a pan and sauté the carrot for 2 minutes. Add the spring onions and sauté until the carrot is tender. Add the cooked arame and the finely grated ginger and stir well together. Season with soya sauce. Set aside in a bowl.

3 To assemble the turnovers for frying, divide the pastry in half and roll out on a lightly floured surface. Then, using a 12 cm bowl or pastry cutter, cut circles of pastry ¼ cm thick. Place one of the pastry circles in front of you. Sprinkle with 1 tsp sesame seeds or sunflower seeds. Place 1 tbsp filling to one side of the circle. Fold pastry over, tucking in any filling that strays out. Seal the edges with a floured fork. The finished turnover will be crescent-shaped. Set aside and repeat until all the filling and pastry is finished. You should have 12 turnovers. Heat the oil in a pot or deep-fat fryer. When the oil is hot, deep-fry the turnovers until brown. This will take about 2 minutes. Fry only 2 or 3 turnovers at a time to give them space to cook evenly.

4 The turnovers are lovely eaten hot or cold. They can be assembled 3–4 hours in advance and fried before serving, or fried in advance and reheated in the oven for 5 or 10 minutes.

TIP: If you don't want to deep-fry the turnovers they can be baked in a preheated oven at Gas 5/190°C/375°F. Bake for 25 minutes until golden brown.

MEDITERRANEAN VEGETABLE AND FETA TURNOVERS, PAGE 31

BHAJIS

Bhajis are a really moreish treat. They're traditionally made with onions, but can be made with any number of very thinly sliced vegetables. Experiment with carrot and sweet potato, below, or combinations of parsnips or squash.

Regardless of what veg you choose, the method is the same. If you don't have a deep-fat fryer, pour 2 inches of oil into a pot to deep-fry the bhajis. Heat the oil. To check if it's hot enough, drop a small piece of bread into the oil; it should drop to the bottom and pop back up to the top of the oil immediately, sizzling furiously.

Spoon heaped dessertspoons (golf-ball sized amounts) of bhaji mix into the hot oil and fry until brown for approx. 3 minutes. Drain on kitchen paper.

TIP: Leave room between the bhajis as they cook; they will fry more evenly. I usually fry 3 at a time. Keep the oven warm and place the cooked bhajis there while you fry the rest.

TIP: I have found that even though frying them and serving straight away is best, this recipe heats up very well the next day in a hot oven (Gas 7/220°C/425°F) – meaning that the cook doesn't have to contend with boiling oil and entertaining at the same time!

Serve with yoghurt and mint dip (p. 107).

ONION BHAJIS

MAKES 12

1 LARGE ONION
150 G GRAM (CHICKPEA) FLOUR
2 TSP FRESH CHILLI, DESEEDED AND FINELY CHOPPED
$1/_2$ TSP TURMERIC
$1/_2$ TSP BAKING POWDER
$1/_2$ TSP GROUND CUMIN
2 TBSP FRESH CORIANDER, CHOPPED
SEA SALT
SUNFLOWER OR PEANUT OIL FOR DEEP-FRYING

1 In a large bowl, place the gram flour, chilli, turmeric, baking powder, and cumin. Peel and halve the onion and slice into half moon shapes. Mix well with all the other ingredients. Add the coriander to the mix along with 200 ml water. Mix thoroughly and season with sea salt. Follow the method above to shape and fry the bhajis.

SWEET POTATO AND CARROT BHAJIS

My children and their friends love these bhajis – I think it's the natural sweetness and the great colour that does it.

MAKES 12

150 G SWEET POTATO
85 G CARROT
150 G GRAM (CHICKPEA) FLOUR
1 TSP FRESH CHILLI, DESEEDED AND MINCED
$1/_2$ TSP TURMERIC
$1/_2$ TSP BAKING POWDER
$1/_2$ TSP GROUND CUMIN
2 TBSP FRESH CORIANDER, CHOPPED
SEA SALT
SUNFLOWER OIL OR PEANUT OIL, FOR DEEP FRYING

1 Peel the sweet potato and chop into 4 cm long pieces and julienne. Prepare the carrot in the same way. In a large bowl, place the gram flour, chilli, turmeric, baking powder, and cumin. Add the carrot and sweet potato and mix well. Add the coriander to the mix along with 200 ml water. Mix thoroughly and season with sea salt. Follow the method above to shape and fry the bhajis.

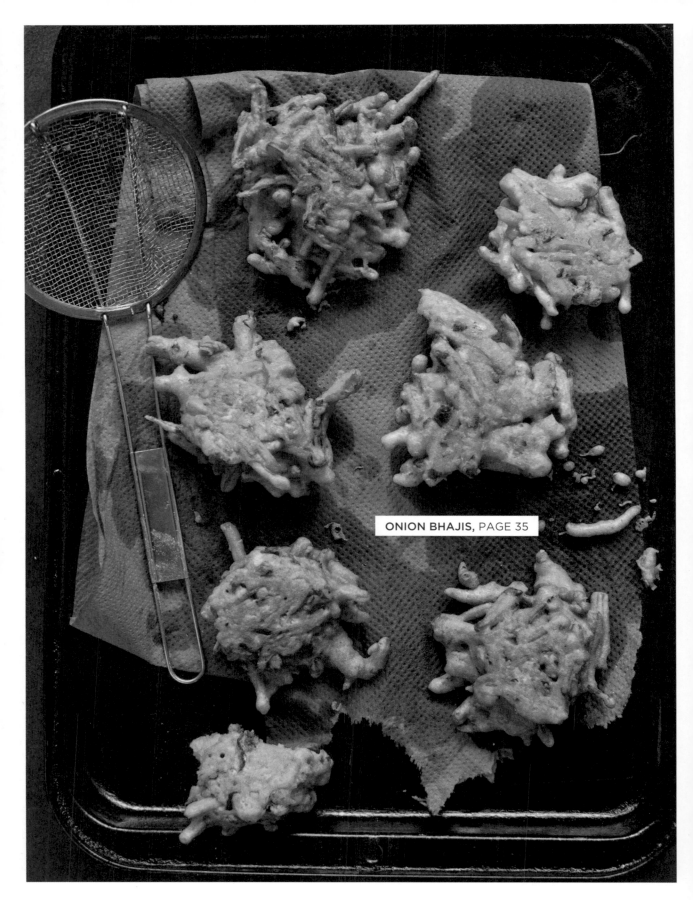

ONION BHAJIS, PAGE 35

Paddy's
Choice
feb 2014

SWEET POTATO AND CARROT BHAJIS, PAGE 35

THE MUCH-MALIGNED VEGGIE BURGER

Veggie burgers are omnipresent, but all too often are frozen, bland patties of unidentifiable brown mush with the odd kidney bean or corn kernel poking out. We can do better! These veggie patties are delicious, filling and worthy of the name 'burger'. Like their meaty counterparts, these burgers demand traditional BBQ accompaniments of slaw (pages 18–19) and potato salads (pages, 12–13), along with some leafy greens.

BUCKWHEAT BURGERS WITH NORI AND SPINACH

MAKES 6
150 G BUCKWHEAT
½ ONION, SLICED
SOYA SAUCE
25 G CARROT, ROUGHLY GRATED

25 G BABY SPINACH LEAVES
15 G TOASTED PUMPKIN SEEDS
1 TSP FRESH GINGER, FINELY GRATED
1 SHEET NORI SEAWEED

1 Using a heavy-bottomed pot, bring 375 ml water to a boil. Rinse the buckwheat, and drain. Add to the boiling water, along with the sliced onion and 2 tbsp soya sauce. Bring back to a boil, cover tightly, lower the heat and simmer for 30 minutes.

2 Stir the cooked buckwheat and place into a large bowl. Cut the sheet of nori into three strips, and slice the strips into thin pieces. Add the roughly grated carrot, baby spinach leaves, nori, pumpkin seeds and ginger. Stir well, allowing the spinach leaves to wilt in the warm buckwheat. Taste and season with soya sauce. Divide the burgers into 6 portions. With dampened hands, shape the buckwheat portions into burger. Place in the fridge to set and chill.

3 To fry the burgers, heat 2 tbsp unrefined sunflower oil in a pan. Fry the burgers on both sides until brown.

SERVE WITH TOMATO AND RED ONION SALSA:
4 TOMATOES
1 SMALL RED ONION, FINELY DICED
1 TSP CHILLI, FINELY CHOPPED

2 TSP FRESH CORIANDER, FINELY CHOPPED
LEMON JUICE
SEA SALT

1 Remove green stems from the tomatoes. Cut a small x into the top of each tomato, and place in a bowl of boiling water for 2 minutes. Rinse under cold water. The skins should slide off. Chop the tomatoes into small dice. Place in a bowl with the red onion, chilli, fresh coriander. Season with sea salt and fresh lemon juice. Mix well.

TIP: The burgers are best made the day before or at least 3–4 hours before serving, as it allows them to set better.

BUCKWHEAT BURGERS WITH NORI AND SPINACH

COUSCOUS, BUTTERBEAN AND MUSHROOM BURGERS

COUSCOUS, BUTTERBEAN AND MUSHROOM BURGERS

MAKES 6
250 G WHOLEMEAL COUSCOUS
100 G COOKED BUTTERBEANS
300 G BUTTON MUSHROOMS
50 G BREADCRUMBS
30 ML BALSAMIC VINEGAR
1 TSP RED CHILLI, DESEEDED AND FINELY CHOPPED
1 CLOVE GARLIC, MINCED
25 G FRESH CORIANDER, CHOPPED
SEA SALT
SUNFLOWER OIL FOR FRYING

1 Wash the couscous, cover with water and leave to soak in a bowl for 1 hour. Thinly slice the mushrooms and sauté in a frying pan with a small pinch of salt until cooked. Place in a colander and drain off the juices. Pulse cooked mushrooms in a food processor until finely chopped, and empty into a large bowl. Blend the cooked butter beans in a food processor until smooth, and add to the mushrooms along with the soaked couscous, breadcrumbs, balsamic vinegar, chilli, garlic and coriander. Season with sea salt.

2 Mix well until all the ingredients are blended well together. Taste the mix and adjust the seasoning if needed. Divide the mix into 6 portions. Dampen your hands with water and shape the portions into a burger shape. Heat the sunflower oil in a frying pan and heat over a medium heat. Fry the burgers on each side until crisp and golden.

3 Serve with salsa on p. 38, in a bun or in pitta bread with yoghurt mint sauce (p. 109).

TIP: If you want to serve these burgers in bread I find they work better in a pitta pocket than a burger bun, because it complements the flavour of the burger and is less messy with the sauces and salad. If serving this way, divide the mix into 9 or 12 instead of 6 and follow the same method as above.

MILLET, SWEET POTATO AND CASHEW BURGERS

MAKES 6
150 G MILLET
150 G SWEET POTATO
150 G CAULIFLOWER
SEA SALT
25 G TOASTED CASHEWS
25 G CARROT, ROUGHLY GRATED
25 G SUNFLOWER SEEDS, TOASTED
1/2 TSP GINGER, GRATED FINE
1/2 TSP GROUND CUMIN
2 TSP FRESH PARSLEY, CHOPPED
SOYA SAUCE
SUNFLOWER OIL FOR FRYING

1 Wash the millet well, drain and place in a heavy-bottomed pot. Peel and chop the sweet potato into 1 cm cubes. Divide the cauliflower into florets. Add both to the millet in the pot with a pinch of salt and 300 ml water. Cover and bring to a boil. Lower the heat, (use a flame cover if you have one), and simmer for 30 minutes.

2 When the millet and vegetables are cooked, stir. The vegetables will blend well into the millet. Transfer into a large bowl. Roughly chop the cashew nuts. Add to the millet along with the grated carrot, sunflower seeds, ginger, cumin powder, parsley and 2 tsp soya sauce. Mix well. Season with sea salt. Divide the mix into 6 portions. With dampened hands, shape the portions into burgers. Place in the fridge to set for about 2 hours.

3 Heat 2 tbsp sunflower oil in a pan. Fry the burgers on both sides until golden brown. Serve with salsa (p. 38) or pesto (p. 54).

TIP: The burgers are best made the day before or at least 3–4 hours before serving, as it allows them to set better.

RED LENTIL AND BROWN RICE BURGERS

MAKES 6
300 G RED LENTILS
375 G COOKED ORGANIC BROWN BASMATI RICE
1 TSP RED CHILLI, DESEEDED AND MINCED
2 TBSP FRESH CORIANDER
2 TBSP RED ONION, FINELY DICED
SEA SALT
SUNFLOWER OIL, FOR FRYING

1 Wash the lentils until the water runs clear. Place in a heavy-bottomed pot with 450 ml water. Cover and bring to a boil on a medium heat, then reduce the heat to a simmer and cook until all the lentils are cooked and mushy, 25–30 minutes. It is important to stir the lentils constantly as they can stick to the bottom of the pot very easily. Do not salt until cooking is finished as salt can slow the cooking time of beans.

2 Place the lentils into a large bowl and add the cooked rice, chilli, red onion and coriander. Season with salt. Divide into 6 portions. Dampen your hands and shape the mix into burgers. Place in the fridge to chill and set.

3 Heat sunflower oil in a frying pan over a medium heat and fry the burgers until golden brown on both sides.

4 Serve with salsa, p. 38.

5 These burgers will keep refrigerated for 3–4 days.

TIP: If you're making these burgers for children, consider reducing the amount of chilli, or omitting it entirely. Divide the mix into 10 portions. This size is also perfect for serving the burgers in pitta bread with salad.

TIP: 150 g of raw brown basmati rice with 385 ml of water should give you 375 g of cooked rice.

BRUNCH

Brunch is great meal to get creative with when the full Irish gives way to some more interesting and indulgent dishes. There is something for everyone in this brunch menu, with sweet, savoury and spicy flavours for a lazy start to a weekend.

SWEETCORN PANCAKES

These pancakes also make a very good starter, or serve with soup for a wholesome bread-free lunch. Accompany with spicy, finely chopped avocado and pico de gallo salad, p. 4.

MAKES 12 PANCAKES
115 G WHITE SPELT OR WHITE PLAIN FLOUR
40 G FINE POLENTA (CORNMEAL)
¹/₂ TSP BAKING POWDER
125 G SWEETCORN
SEA SALT
1 TBSP SPRING ONION, FINELY CHOPPED
1 FREE RANGE EGG, BEATEN
125 ML CRÈME FRAÎCHE OR THICK YOGHURT
100 ML MILK, ENOUGH TO FORM A SMOOTH THICK BATTER

1 In a large bowl, sift the flour, salt and baking powder. Stir in the cornmeal, and the spring onion. Make a well in the centre and pour in the beaten egg and crème fraîche and whisk until smooth. Continue to whisk in enough milk to make a thick, smooth batter. Stir in the sweet corn and leave to rest for 10 minutes.

2 Heat a frying pan over a medium heat. Heat 1 tbsp sunflower oil. Using a tablespoon, spoon 3 or 4 pancakes onto the hot pan. When golden brown, approx. 3 minutes, turn over and cook the other side.

3 Serve warm.

SPINACH AND GOAT'S CHEESE MUFFINS

MAKES 12
4 FREE RANGE EGGS
100 G SUNFLOWER MARGARINE OR SOFTENED BUTTER

100 G SOFT GOAT'S CHEESE
55 G VEGETARIAN PARMESAN-STYLE CHEESE
140 G SPINACH OR BABY SPINACH LEAVES
1/4 TSP PAPRIKA
350 G WHITE SPELT FLOUR
2 TSP BAKING POWDER
1/2 TSP SEA SALT
250 G NATURAL YOGHURT

1 Preheat oven to Gas 3/170°C/325°F.

2 Heat the oven. Oil and line a 12-cup muffin tray with paper cases. Lightly oil the paper cases.

3 In a large bowl, whisk the eggs with the margarine. Add the yoghurt and stir. Rinse the spinach well and slice finely. Add to the bowl. Mix the flour, baking powder, salt and paprika together and sift into the egg and spinach mix. Mix well. Finely grate the Parmesan-style cheese into the mix.

4 Spoon the mix into the muffin cups, half-filling the cups. Divide the goat's cheese equally between the muffins, placing a small amount in each cup. Spoon the remainder of the muffin mix on top of the goat's cheese. Place tray in the centre of the preheated oven for 30 minutes until the muffins are baked through.

TIP: If the goat's cheese you're using has a rind, use 125 g so that you have 100 g cheese after you remove the rind.

POLENTA GEMS

These little muffins are light and delicious. They have the nutty flavour and crunch of the polenta. Serve with soup, salad or stews.

MAKES 18
55 G UNSALTED BUTTER
90 G POLENTA
140 G WHITE SPELT OR PLAIN FLOUR

2 TSP BAKING POWDER
1 FREE RANGE EGG
200G NATURAL YOGHURT
1 TBSP AGAVE OR MAPLE SYRUP

1 Preheat oven to Gas 3/170°C/325°F.

2 Oil 2 muffin tins. I use a muffin tray with shallow cups, (2 cm deep), but a standard muffin tray is fine. Place the butter in a bowl in the oven to melt. Place the polenta and the white spelt flour and the baking powder into a large bowl and mix well. Make a well in the centre and break the egg into it. Add the yoghurt and whisk in the milk and agave syrup. Take the now melted butter out of the oven and whisk in until all the ingredients are combined and the batter smooth. Spoon into the 18 oiled muffin cups. The mix will not come to the top of the cups. Bake in the middle of the preheated oven for 10–12 minutes until the gems are springy to the touch. Cool for a few minutes in the trays on a wire rack. Using a knife, remove the gems carefully from the trays and cool fully on the wire rack.

TIP: These can be stored in an airtight container for 3–4 days.

TOFU FRENCH TOAST

This is very popular with children, vegetarians and vegans alike. It's a great way to use up not-so-fresh bread.

SERVES 2
125 G CUBE TOFU
20 ML SOYA SAUCE
40 ML WATER
SUNFLOWER OIL
2 LARGE SLICES SOURDOUGH BREAD
ORGANIC MAPLE SYRUP

1 Place the tofu into the jug of a hand blender. Add 20 ml soya sauce and 40 ml water. Blend until smooth. Pour onto a flat dish. Heat 2 tbsp sunflower oil in a frying pan over a medium heat. Slice the sourdough bread in half on the diagonal.

2 When the pan is hot, dip the bread into the tofu and soya sauce mix and coat both sides of the bread. Fry on both sides until brown. Serve drizzled with organic maple syrup.

TIP: Use a knife or spoon to spread the tofu evenly onto the last piece of bread.

PIZZA

To an Italian, pizza isn't junk food. Homemade pizza is wholesome, nutritious and makes a great family meal, especially if it's made by all the family. Little ones can do the toppings, and teenage angst can be worked out in the kneading. Naturally, making it yourself means that you can go for any combination of flavours that you like, or do different toppings on different sections to keep everyone happy.

PIZZA SAUCE

MAKES FIVE 25CM PIZZAS
EXTRA VIRGIN OLIVE OIL
1 SMALL ONION, FINELY CHOPPED
2 CLOVES GARLIC, MINCED
1 400G TIN CHOPPED TOMATOES
200 ML PASSATA
SEA SALT
1 TSP DRIED BASIL OR OREGANO OR ITALIAN HERBS
2 TSP FRESH BASIL, CHOPPED
COARSELY GROUND BLACK PEPPER

Heat 2 tbsp olive oil in a pot. Sauté the onion and garlic for 2 minutes. Add the tomatoes, passata, 200ml water, a good pinch of sea salt and 1 tsp of dried basil. Bring to a boil, lower the heat and simmer until it reduces to a thick sauce. This will take about 20–25 minutes. Add fresh basil and season.

PIZZA BASES

MAKES FIVE 25 CM BASES
3 TSP FRESH YEAST
2 TBSP EXTRA VIRGIN OLIVE OIL
300 ML LUKEWARM WATER
500 G WHOLEMEAL SPELT FLOUR
1/2 TSP SEA SALT

1 Place the fresh yeast, olive oil and lukewarm water into a large mixing bowl and whisk together. Leave to stand for 5 minutes to allow the yeast to activate.

2 Add the flour and the sea salt. Using your hands, bring everything together. Turn out onto a floured surface and knead for 10 minutes. The dough will become soft and smooth. Form the dough into a ball and place in a lightly oiled mixing bowl, turning once to oil the dough. Cover with cling film and leave in a warm place for 1 hour to double in size.

3 Preheat oven to Gas 4/180°C/350°F.

4 Turn the risen dough out onto a clean surface. Punch the dough back and divide into 5 equal pieces. Take each dough piece and knead on a floured surface for a few minutes. With a floured rolling pin, roll out the dough to a 25 cm round base. Place on an oiled baking sheet. Allow to rise for 5 minutes. Bake on the top shelf of a preheated oven for 10 minutes. The base is now ready.

5 Top with pizza sauce and toppings of your choice and return to the oven to bake.

TIP: These pizza bases freeze very well. After baking the base, cool and wrap in greaseproof paper and aluminium foil and place in the freezer. To use a frozen pizza base, unwrap and heat in a moderate oven for 3 minutes before adding sauce and toppings.

TIP: When I can't get fresh yeast, I have used Dove's Farm quick yeast. It works really well, particularly if you're making the pizza dough to use for turnovers (pages 30–32). If using quick yeast, use only 1 tsp. Stir the yeast straight into the flour with the salt, olive oil and lukewarm water. Follow the method above for kneading and proving.

TIP: Some people feel that a little white flour makes the base lighter. Here are some measurements below to try. Follow the method above.

3 TSP FRESH YEAST
2 TBSP EXTRA VIRGIN OLIVE OIL
300 ML LUKEWARM WATER
375 G WHOLEMEAL SPELT FLOUR
125 G WHITE SPELT FLOUR
1/2 TSP SEA SALT

MOZZARELLA PIZZA WITH ROASTED PEPPERS, COURGETTE AND PESTO

MAKES ONE 25CM PIZZA
1 25 CM WHOLEMEAL PIZZA BASE (P. 52)
PIZZA SAUCE (P. 51)
½ PEPPER
½ COURGETTE
EXTRA VIRGIN OLIVE OIL
SEA SALT
85 G MOZZARELLA CHEESE, GRATED

FOR THE PESTO:
15 G PINE NUTS
15 G SUNFLOWER SEEDS
55 G FRESH BASIL LEAVES
1 CLOVE OF GARLIC, CHOPPED
SEA SALT
125 ML UNREFINED SUNFLOWER OIL
250 ML EXTRA VIRGIN OLIVE OIL
25 G VEGETARIAN PARMESAN-STYLE CHEESE

1 Preheat the oven to Gas 7/220°C/425°F.

2 Thinly slice the pepper and julienne the courgette. Place on a baking sheet. Drizzle with 2 tsp olive oil and a pinch of salt and toss well to coat the vegetables. Roast on the top shelf of the oven for 15 minutes. Set aside.

3 Place the pizza base on a flat baking tray. (If it frozen, thaw in the preheated oven for 1 minute.) Spread 3 tbsp pizza sauce over pizza base, spreading it out to the edges. Sprinkle with mozzarella, and lay the roasted red pepper and julienned courgette evenly over the cheese. Bake on the top shelf of the preheated oven for 20–25 minutes.

4 While the pizza is baking, make the pesto. Place the pine nuts and sunflower seeds into a pan and toast until golden brown. Blend in a food processor with the fresh basil, a pinch of sea salt the garlic. Pulse into a coarse paste. Mix the oils together and, with, the motor running, pour the oil slowly into the feeder tube of the food processor and blend. Empty pesto into a bowl and stir in finely grated Parmesan-style cheese. Season with sea salt.

5 When the cheese on the pizza has melted and is golden brown in places, remove from the oven and drizzle with basil pesto. Delicious hot or cold.

TIP: To make a quick basil oil instead of the pesto, finely chop basil leaves and mix with extra virgin olive oil and season with a little sea salt.

TIP: To make this pizza vegan, omit the cheese. Blend 1 cube of tofu with 1 tsp soya sauce. If it is too thick, add a little water and season again with soya sauce. Follow the recipe above, replacing the grated mozzarella with the tofu mix. Bake until the tofu has set and has turned brown in places, about 25–30 minutes. Omit the cheese from the pesto and drizzle over the cooked pizza. This pizza will be enjoyed by everyone – not just vegans. Try it out!

SPINACH, RED ONION AND GOAT'S CHEESE PIZZA

MAKES ONE 25CM PIZZA
1 25 CM WHOLEMEAL PIZZA BASE (P. 52)
PIZZA SAUCE (P. 51)
70 G BABY SPINACH LEAVES
1 SMALL RED ONION

EXTRA VIRGIN OLIVE OIL
SEA SALT
115 G SEMI-SOFT GOAT'S CHEESE, END RIND REMOVED
COARSELY GROUND BLACK PEPPER

1 Preheat oven to Gas 7/220°C/425°F.

2 Rinse the spinach and shake the water from the leaves. Place them in a large bowl. Peel and cut the red onion in half and slice into half-moon pieces. Separate the pieces of onion and put into the bowl with the spinach leaves. Add 1 tsp olive oil, a small pinch of sea salt, and toss well to coat the vegetables.

3 Place the pizza base on a flat baking tray. (If it frozen, thaw in the preheated oven for 1 minute.) Spread 3 tbsp pizza sauce over pizza base, spreading it out to the edges. Scatter the spinach and red onion evenly onto the pizza.

4 Thinly slice or crumble the goat's cheese over the pizza, and season with pepper.

5 Bake on the top shelf of the preheated oven for 20 minutes or until the goat's cheese has begun to brown and the spinach leaves have wilted. Delicious hot or cold.

TIP: The goat's cheese can be replaced with feta cheese.

TIP: For a bit of a kick, sprinkle lightly with dried chilli flakes.

PUMPKIN, SAGE AND RICOTTA PIZZA

MAKES ONE 25CM PIZZA
1 25 CM WHOLEMEAL PIZZA BASE (P. 52)
400G PUMPKIN OR BUTTERNUT SQUASH
EXTRA VIRGIN OLIVE OIL
SEA SALT
100G RICOTTA CHEESE

2 CLOVES GARLIC
25G VEGETARIAN PARMESAN-STYLE CHEESE, FINELY GRATED
1 SPRIG FRESH THYME
1 SPRIG FRESH SAGE

1 Peel and thinly slice the pumpkin or butternut squash, approx ¼ cm.

2 Lay the pieces onto a baking tray and season with a little sea salt and drizzle with olive oil. Bake on the top shelf of a preheated hot oven for 15 minutes until the pumpkin is tender. Remove from the oven and set aside. Spread the ricotta cheese over the pizza base, bringing it out to the edges of the base. Lay the baked pumpkin slices on top, overlapping them a little. Thinly slice the cloves of garlic and sprinkle on top of the pumpkin. Sprinkle the Parmesan-style cheese over the pizza. Remove the leaves from the thyme and sage, chop and scatter over the top. Drizzle with a little olive oil and bake on the top shelf of the preheated oven for 20 minutes.

Soups

Blazing Salads made its name on, well, salads, but we've built a real following for our soups, too. We always have three soups on offer at the deli, one of which is always miso. One night, after I arrived in New York, sick and exhausted after a long flight, the miso soup I got around the corner from my hotel somehow made everything better – a nourishing, comforting cure-all.

We put the same energy into all of our soups, whether they're a quick lunch on the hop, a starter or a mealful in a bowl. In little more than half an hour, you'll be ready for a few of those nights when you don't know who will be in for dinner or what you've got in the house to take to the office for lunch.

The best bit about soups is that they're not too fussy if you have extra carrots or you're short on split peas.
Make these recipes your own.

ITALIAN WHITE BEAN AND VEGETABLE SOUP

This soup is filled with great herbs, and Parmesan cheese to add extra depth of flavour.

SERVES 6
1 MEDIUM ONION, DICED
3 CLOVES GARLIC, MINCED
EXTRA VIRGIN OLIVE OIL
2 STICKS CELERY, SLICED
2 MEDIUM CARROTS, DICED
2 MEDIUM COURGETTE, DICED
2 400 G TINS CHOPPED TOMATOES
1 BAY LEAF
DRIED BASIL, TO TASTE
2 SAGE LEAVES
1 SPRIG FRESH ROSEMARY
2 400 G TINS BUTTER BEANS, OR 700 G FRESHLY COOKED BUTTER BEANS
VEGETARIAN PARMESAN-STYLE CHEESE
SEA SALT
COARSE GROUND BLACK PEPPER
FRESH PARSLEY

1 Heat 1 tbsp olive oil in a large pot, then add the onion and sauté until soft. Add the garlic and celery and sauté for a further 2 minutes. Add the carrots, courgette, tomatoes, bay leaf, sage, basil and rosemary. Add 1 litre water and a pinch of salt. Bring to a boil, lower the heat, cover and simmer for 20 minutes.

2 Rinse and drain 1 tin of beans and blend until smooth. Rinse and drain the other tin and leave whole. Add both lots of beans to the soup and stir well. Season with salt and pepper and garnish with plenty of finely chopped fresh parsley and finely grated Parmesan.

TIP: Serve with rosemary croutons for extra flavour and crunch. Chop 2 slices of white sourdough or baguette into 2 cm cubes. Place on an ovenproof dish and add 1 tablespoon of extra virgin olive oil. Chop 1 small sprig of fresh rosemary and add to the cubed bread and olive oil and toss well. Place on the top shelf of a hot oven (Gas 7/220°C/425°F). Bake for 10 minutes until the bread has become crunchy. This is a great way to use up stale bread. Keep in an airtight container and sprinkle on salads too.

MEDITERRANEAN ROASTED AUBERGINE SOUP

One of the most popular soups in the deli, this has a smooth, creamy texture and lovely richness.

SERVES 6
4 AUBERGINES
2 RED ONIONS
400 G CELERIAC
2 PARSNIPS
4 CLOVES GARLIC
1 TIN CHOPPED OR WHOLE TOMATOES
EXTRA VIRGIN OLIVE OIL
2 TSP PAPRIKA
1 TBSP FRESH ROSEMARY, CHOPPED
1 TSP DRIED BASIL
1 TSP DRIED OREGANO
SEA SALT

1 Preheat oven to Gas 7/220°C/425°F.

2 Chop the aubergine into 2½cm pieces. Chop the red onion. Slice 2 cloves of garlic. Place all three in an ovenproof dish. Add paprika, rosemary and a good pinch of salt. Toss in 2 tbsp olive oil. Place on the top shelf of the hot oven and roast for 20 minutes, until the aubergine is soft.

3 While the aubergine and onion are roasting, peel and chop the celeriac and parsnip into 2½cm pieces. Heat some olive oil in a large pot, add the celeriac and parsnip and 2 cloves of minced garlic and sauté until the edges of the vegetables become golden. Add 1 tin tomatoes, basil, oregano, a pinch of salt and 1½ litres water. Bring to a boil, cover and simmer for 20 minutes until the vegetables are soft. When all the vegetables are cooked, add the roasted aubergine and red onion to the pot of celeriac and parsnip. Blend until smooth and season with salt and pepper.

CHUNKY POTATO AND CORN SOUP

This soup is perfect comfort food for a cold day. The thyme and bay leaf add a peppery and autumnal seasoning to the soup.

SERVES 6
SUNFLOWER OIL OR EXTRA VIRGIN OLIVE OIL
1 ONION, DICED
1 LARGE CLOVE OF GARLIC, MINCED
1 STICK CELERY, DICED
4 FLOURY POTATOES, ABOUT 400 G
150 G SWEETCORN
2 TSP FRESH THYME, MINCED
1 BAY LEAF
SEA SALT
COARSELY GROUND BLACK PEPPER
1 TBSP FRESH PARSLEY, FINELY CHOPPED

1 In a large pot heat 1 tbsp of sunflower oil over a medium heat. Sauté the onion for 3 minutes. Add the garlic and the celery and sauté for a further 3 minutes. Peel and dice the potatoes. Add to the pot along with the sweetcorn, thyme, bay leaf and a good pinch of salt. Pour in 1 litre water, bring to a boil, lower the heat and simmer for 20 minutes. Check the potatoes and give them extra cooking time if needed. Add boiled water to reach the consistency of soup you like. Season with salt and pepper and garnish with chopped parsley.

MOROCCAN SOUPS

Moroccan food is perhaps best known for its intensely aromatic, slow-cooked tagines. By roasting the spices for these soups, you can recreate those same exotic flavours for these one-pot speedy soups.

MOROCCAN MINESTRONE

This soup was adapted from the classic Italian minestrone. Most one-pot dishes can be given a makeover by simply changing the herbs and spices – be adventurous! (See photos, page 66.)

SERVES 6
EXTRA VIRGIN OLIVE OIL
1 ONION, DICED
1 CLOVE GARLIC, MINCED
½ INCH PIECE GINGER
1 TSP GROUND CUMIN
½ TSP TURMERIC
1 400 G TIN CHOPPED TOMATOES
200 G PASSATA (SIEVED TOMATOES)
1 BAY LEAF
2 STICKS CELERY, SLICED
2 MEDIUM CARROTS, DICED
1 MEDIUM COURGETTE, DICED
SEA SALT
1 HANDFUL WHOLEMEAL SPELT PENNE OR FUSILLI
2 TBSP CHICKPEAS, COOKED
1 TBSP FRESH CORIANDER, CHOPPED
2 TSP FRESH PARSLEY, CHOPPED

1 Heat 2 tbsp olive oil in a large pot. Sauté the onion for 2 minutes, add the garlic and ginger and sauté for a further 1 minute. Add the cumin and turmeric to the pot and sauté for 1 minute more. Stir in the chopped tomatoes, passata, celery, carrots, courgette and the bay leaf and a good pinch of sea salt. Pour in 1 litre water, cover and bring to a boil. Lower the heat to a simmer and cook for 10 minutes. Add 1 handful of pasta and cook for a further 10 minutes. Stir in the chickpeas, fresh coriander and fresh parsley. Check the seasoning.

TIP: Use any wholemeal pasta in this recipe, just remember that wholemeal wheat pasta takes longer to cook than wholemeal spelt pasta.

TIP: Serve with toasted fingers of sourdough bread spread with tapenade – so good.

MOROCCAN LENTIL AND VEGETABLE

See photo on the following page.

SERVES 6
175 G RED LENTILS
55 G PUY LENTILS
EXTRA VIRGIN OLIVE OIL
1 MEDIUM ONION, DICED
1 CARROT, DICED
1 STICK CELERY, DICED
1/2 RED PEPPER, DICED
1 TSP CUMIN SEEDS
1/2 TSP CORIANDER SEEDS
PINCH TURMERIC
2 CLOVES GARLIC, MINCED
1/2 RED CHILLI, DESEEDED AND CHOPPED FINE
2 TSP FRESH GINGER, FINELY GRATED
200 G CHOPPED TINNED TOMATOES
1 TBSP FRESH CORIANDER, CHOPPED
SEA SALT

1 Place the cumin and coriander seeds into a dry pan and toast over a medium heat for 5 minutes until lightly toasted. Grind in a mortar and pestle or clean coffee grinder. Wash the lentils several times in cold water to clean them.

2 In a large pot heat the olive oil over a medium heat and sauté the onion for 2 minutes. Add the garlic and sauté for 1 minute. Then add the ginger, chilli, turmeric and the freshly ground coriander and cumin and sauté for a further minute. Add the carrot, celery, red pepper and tomato and stir. Place the washed lentils on top. Pour in 1½ litres cold water and add a pinch of salt. Cover and bring to a boil, lower the heat and simmer for 30 minutes. When the soup is cooked stir well, season with salt and pepper and stir in the coriander. Add hot water to reach desired thickness, and serve.

MOROCCAN MINESTRONE, PAGE 64

MOROCCAN LENTIL AND VEGETABLE, PAGE 65

UKRAINIAN BORSCHT WITH HARICOT BEANS

This recipe came from Zenon, a Polish chef in the deli. Though it originates in Ukraine, it is popular recipe in Poland, and a version of this is traditionally served at Christmas Eve feasts.

SERVES 6
1 ONION, DICED
1 CLOVE GARLIC, MINCED
2 CARROTS, DICED
2 POTATOES, PEELED AND DICED
1 SMALL PARSNIP, DICED
CELERIAC, PEELED AND DICED, (SAME AMOUNT AS PARSNIP)
4 MEDIUM RAW BEETROOTS
1 400G TIN HARICOT BEANS, OR 350G OF FRESH COOKED HARICOT BEANS
3 PIMENTOS
1 BAY LEAF
2 TSP FRESH MARJORAM OR 1 TSP OF DRIED MARJORAM
LEMON JUICE TO TASTE
1 TBSP APPLE CONCENTRATE
SEA SALT
COARSELY GROUND BLACK PEPPER

1 In a large pot, sauté the onion in a little olive oil to soften. Add the garlic and sauté for a few minutes more. Add the carrots and 1 litre water, bring to a boil. Add the potatoes, parsnip, celeriac, pimentos, bay leaf, marjoram and sea salt. Lower the heat, cover and simmer for 15 minutes.

2 Peel and roughly grate the raw beetroot and add to the pot along with the cooked haricots. Cook for a further 10 minutes. Check that the vegetables are tender. Add the apple concentrate. Season with salt, pepper and lemon juice for a balanced sweet-and-sour taste.

3 Serve with a dollop of crème fraîche or tofu sour cream.

SOUPS WITH WINTER GREENS

Kale, savoy cabbage, leaf spinach, mustard greens and many more sturdy winter greens grow well in Ireland and have always been a part of our culinary heritage. If you have an allotment or a seasonal vegetable delivery service, you'll no doubt have wondered what to do with a fridgeful of them in the late winter. It's important to remember that all of these leafy veg are interchangeable, so use whichever you like best or whatever you've got to hand, and don't be afraid to adjust the seasoning to suit.

POTATO AND KALE SOUP

This is a creamy soup with a light earthy flavour for a warming meal. Serve with garlic bread for extra kick.

SERVES 6
UNREFINED SUNFLOWER OIL
2 ONIONS, DICED
2 CLOVES GARLIC
1½ KG FLOURY POTATOES
SEA SALT
FRESH THYME
1 MEDIUM CARROT
2 KALE LEAVES (LARGE LEAVES)
COARSE GROUND BLACK PEPPER

1 Heat 2 tbsp sunflower oil in a pot. Add the onion and sauté for 3 minutes. Add the garlic and sauté for 1 minute more. Remove from the heat. Peel and chop the potatoes. Add to the pot with a good pinch of sea salt, the leaves from a small sprig of fresh thyme, and 1½ litres water. Put a lid on top, bring to a boil and simmer for 25 minutes.

2 Roughly grate the carrot. Remove the thick stem from the kale leaves and shred finely. Heat 1 tbsp sunflower oil in a pan and add the carrot and the kale, a pinch of sea salt and sauté until cooked. To cook the kale fully, add water to the pan, a spoonful at a time. Cooking time should take about 10 minutes, or half that if you are using young kale leaves. Use the stems of the young kale leaves also as they will be nice and tender.

3 When the soup is cooked, blend until smooth. Stir in the sautéed carrot and kale. Add boiling water to desired thickness. Season with sea salt and pepper.

MUSHROOM, SAVOY CABBAGE AND BARLEY SOUP

This is a meal in itself with a nice hunk of rye sourdough bread.

SERVES 6
UNREFINED SUNFLOWER OIL
1 ONION, FINELY DICED
2 CELERY STICKS, FINELY DICED
1 CLOVE GARLIC, MINCED
2 MEDIUM CARROTS, FINELY DICED
3 KALE LEAVES, STALKS REMOVED AND CHOPPED
FRESH THYME
2 BAY LEAVES
125 G BARLEY
SEA SALT
1 LARGE PORTOBELLO MUSHROOM
200 G BUTTON MUSHROOMS
SOYA SAUCE
FRESH PARSLEY

1 Heat 1 tbsp sunflower oil in a large pot and sauté the onion for 2 minutes. Add the celery and garlic and sauté for 1 minute more. Add the carrot, kale, thyme, bay leaves, barley and a pinch of sea salt. Pour in 1½ litres water. Cover, bring to a boil, and simmer for 40 minutes.

2 While the soup is cooking, chop the Portobello mushroom finely and slice the button mushrooms. Heat 1 tbsp sunflower in a pan, add the mushrooms and sauté until the mushroom slices begin to brown. Season with sea salt and 1 tsp fresh thyme. When the soup is cooked, add the cooked mushrooms. Season with soya sauce to taste and chopped fresh parsley.

Add boiling water to reach the desired thickness and adjust the seasoning with soya sauce.

TIP: Miso works very well in replace of the soya sauce. Blend the miso with a little soup stock in a bowl, then add to the pot gradually to taste.

SPLIT PEA SOUPS

Split peas come in green, of course, and bright, sunny yellow. Either colour, or a combination of them, works for these recipes, though if you're puréeing the soup, stick to one colour. They are available dried in supermarkets, health food shops and even some convenience stores. In Indian and south Asian shops, they're often sold very cheaply in large quantities, and labelled as 'tarka daal', and used to make daal, a nourishing staple of Indian vegetarian cooking. These three very different soups show how versatile split peas can be, and how they're a great thing to keep stashed in the back of your press.

To prepare the peas, wash well in a basin of water, drain, and place in a pot with 1½ litres water. Bring to a boil and simmer until cooked, about 1 hour. When cooking the split peas, stir regularly, as they can stick to the base of the pot. A froth can come to the top of the pot at the start of cooking; just scoop off with a spoon. Do not add salt as it will prevent the peas from softening.

GREEN SPLIT PEA AND BARLEY SOUP

SERVES 6
55 G BARLEY, SOAKED OVERNIGHT OR FOR 6–8 HOURS
500 G YELLOW OR GREEN SPLIT PEAS
UNREFINED SUNFLOWER OIL
1 ONION, DICED
1 STICK CELERY, SLICED
1 MEDIUM CARROT, DICED
1 MEDIUM PARSNIP, DICED
TURNIP, DICED, SAME AMOUNT AS CARROT
FRESH THYME
1 BAY LEAF
SEA SALT
FRESH PARSLEY, TO GARNISH

1 In a large pot, heat sunflower oil and sauté the onion for 3 minutes. Add the soaked barley, celery, carrot, parsnip, turnip, 2 tsp thyme, the bay leaf and a good pinch of sea salt. Pour in 1 litre water. Put a lid on top, bring to a boil, lower the heat and simmer for 20 minutes.

2 When the yellow split peas are cooked, stir into the cooked vegetable soup. Stir well until the peas and vegetables are well mixed. If the soup is too thick, add some boiling water. Return to the heat, stirring regularly for 5 minutes. Season with salt and garnish with chopped parsley.

TIP: This soup can be blended for a puréed, creamy soup. Just remember to remove the bay leaf before you put it in the food processor.

YELLOW SPLIT PEA SOUP WITH CELERIAC AND PARSNIP

A fragrant soup that makes great use of celeriac, a vegetable that many people just don't know what to do with.

SERVES 6
500 G YELLOW SPLIT PEAS
UNREFINED SUNFLOWER OIL
1 ONION
1 LARGE STICK OF CELERY
2 CLOVES OF GARLIC, MINCED
2 PARSNIPS
750G CELERIAC
1 SPRIG FRESH ROSEMARY
1 BAY LEAF
SEA SALT
COARSELY GROUND BLACK PEPPER
CHOPPED PARSLEY, TO GARNISH

1 In a separate pot heat 2 tbsp sunflower oil. Add the onion and garlic and sauté for 2 minutes. Add the celery and sauté for 1 minute more. Peel the parsnip and celeriac and chop into 1 cm cubes. Add to the pot with the sprig of rosemary and bay leaf and a good pinch of salt. Pour in 500 ml water, cover and bring to a boil. Lower the heat and simmer for 15 minutes.

2 When the peas are cooked, add to the cooked vegetable stock and stir well. Cook the soup on a low heat for 5 minutes. Remove the bay leaf and the stick of the rosemary sprig. If the soup is too thick add boiling water. Season well with sea salt and black pepper and garnish with fresh parsley.

YELLOW SPLIT PEA SOUP WITH TOFU

This is the most popular soup in the deli. The spices lend depth to the creaminess of the yellow splits, and the cubes of chewy tofu add texture.

SERVES 6
1 CUBE TOFU
SUNFLOWER, PEANUT OR SOYA OIL FOR DEEP FRYING
SOY SAUCE
500 G YELLOW SPLIT PEAS
UNREFINED SUNFLOWER OIL
1 ONION, FINELY DICED
1 TEASPOON RED CHILLI, DESEEDED AND FINELY CHOPPED
3 CLOVES GARLIC, FINELY CHOPPED
1 TSP MUSTARD SEEDS
1 TSP CUMIN SEEDS
SEA SALT
1 TBSP FRESH CORIANDER

1 Dice the tofu into 1 cm cubes and place on kitchen paper towel to drain. Heat the oil for deep-frying. When the oil has reached the correct temperature, drop the cubes of tofu into it. Fry until golden, remove and drain on a paper towel. Place in a bowl and toss in 2 tsp soya sauce. Set aside.

2 Heat 2 tbsp sunflower oil in a separate pot. Add the mustard seeds and cumin seeds and allow to fry for 3 minutes. Lower the heat and add the onion, garlic and chilli, and a pinch of salt and sauté until the onion is soft and the TIPs have browned. When the split peas are well cooked and mushy, add the onion and spices. Wash and finely chop the coriander. Use the stems and the leaves. Stir in about 400 ml boiling water until a creamy consistency has been reached. Stir in the fried tofu. Season with salt.

3 If you don't want to deep-fry the tofu, dice it and place it into an ovenproof dish. Toss with 2 tsp unrefined sunflower oil and 2 tsp soya sauce. Place in a preheated oven Gas 7/200°C/400°F and roast for 30 minutes or until the tofu is firm. Turn the tofu a few times during roasting.

Main Dishes

Some people love to flip through cookbooks to get ideas and inspirations for dinners with friends and family, while others get nervous at the thought of putting a hot dinner on the table every night. The main courses in this collection, like the last, are designed to offer something for everyone.

Many of these dishes have certainly worked wonders for me when I entertain, like the tarts and pies, though they may have a few extra steps, or ingredients that are new to you. Just remember that every cook, no matter how seasoned, benefits from practice before company comes — not that your family will complain as they eat the dry run for Sunday dinner! Reading cookbooks can be like getting directions: you learn in the doing, and sometimes it's not until you get there that the route you took makes sense.

On the other hand, some of my all-time favourites are one-pot wonders, which are perfect for beginners of all ages and a real saviour for when we're all stuck for time. All of the recipes encourage creativity, so learn the feel of the dish and then feel free to cook to your own tastes. We've provided for just that in places by giving different variations on key recipes so that you can take advantage of what's in season, what's in stock in your kitchen and whatever you fancy.

SPINACH AND RICOTTA CANNELLONI

If you are cooking for friends and family, this dish will impress. The filling is light and creamy, and with the richness of the tomato sauce, it will have them asking for more.

SERVES 4
12 TUBES OF CANNELLONI
25 G VEGETARIAN-STYLE PARMESAN CHEESE

FOR THE TOMATO SAUCE:
EXTRA VIRGIN OLIVE OIL
1 ONION, DICED
1 CLOVE GARLIC, MINCED
1 CARROT, DICED (APPROX. 85 G)
350 G PASSATA
1/2 TSP DRIED BASIL OR DRIED OREGANO
SEA SALT
COARSELY GROUND BLACK PEPPER

FOR THE FILLING:
500 G SPINACH LEAVES
EXTRA VIRGIN OLIVE OIL
1 ONION, DICED SMALL
SEA SALT
NUTMEG
175 G RICOTTA CHEESE

1 Make the tomato sauce. Heat 2 tbsp olive oil in a pot and add the onion. Cook over a medium heat until the onion is soft but not brown. Add the garlic and the carrot and stir for 30 seconds. Pour in the passata, add the dried basil and a good pinch of sea salt. Pour in 350 ml water. Cover and bring to a boil, lower the heat and simmer for 30 minutes. Blend the sauce and season with sea salt and pepper.

2 Make the filling. Wash the spinach and remove any thick stalks. Chop finely. Heat 2 tbsp olive oil in a large pot and add the onion and cook until the onion is soft, about 3 minutes. Add the garlic and cook for a further minute. Add the spinach. If all the spinach doesn't fit in the pot at first allow part of it to start sweating and gradually add the rest. Add 2 tbsp water, cover and cook the spinach for 10 minutes. Check the spinach as it is cooking, stirring occasionally. When the spinach is cooked place in a colander to drain. Set aside to cool.

3 Place the cooled spinach into a bowl and add the ricotta cheese. Mix well. Season with sea salt. Grate the nutmeg into the spinach mix to taste.

4 Use an oven proof dish 30 x 27cm.

5 Preheat oven to Gas 5/190°C/375°F.

6 To fill the cannelloni tubes I just use my fingers. Take portions of the spinach and ricotta filling and push it into the tubes, filling them fully. Fill all 12 tubes.

7 Pour 1 ladlefull of tomato sauce onto the bottom of the dish. Arrange the filled tubes of cannelloni on top allowing 3 tubes per person. Ladle the tomato sauce over the cannelloni. Finely grate the Parmesan-style cheese and sprinkle over the dish. Bake for 35–40 minutes.

TIP: If using frozen spinach, use 375 g. Defrost and drain in a colander and follow the method above.

POTATO AND CELERIAC GRATIN WITH A TOMATO, RED ONION AND BLACK OLIVE SAUCE

Serve this full-flavoured gratin with a light green salad for a tasty lunch or supper dish.

SERVES 6 TO 8
500 G POTATOES
1 CELERIAC, ABOUT 400 G
1 SMALL CLOVE OF GARLIC, MINCED
200 ML FRESH CREAM
SEA SALT

FOR THE SAUCE:
EXTRA VIRGIN OLIVE OIL
1 RED ONION, DICED
400 G TIN TOMATOES, CHOPPED
70 G STONED BLACK OLIVES
2 TSP CAPERS
25 G VEGETARIAN PARMESAN-STYLE CHEESE

1 Preheat oven to Gas 6/200°C/400°F.

2 Peel the potatoes and slice very thinly. Peel the celeriac and slice very thinly. In a glass or ceramic ovenproof dish, 25 x 17 cm and 5 cm deep, layer half the sliced potatoes, season with sea salt and sprinkle with the garlic. Lay the celeriac slices on top. Season. Lay the rest of the potatoes on top. Season. Pour over the fresh cream. Cover the dish with tin foil and place in the pre-heated oven for 45 minutes to 1 hour.

3 To make the sauce, heat 2 tbsp extra virgin olive oil in a pan. Add the red onion and sauté for a few minutes. Add the tomatoes and season with sea salt. Cook until the sauce reduces a little. Remove from the heat. Roughly chop the olives and add to the sauce along with the capers. Season. When the potato and celeriac is cooked, remove the foil and spread the red onion and olive mix on top. Finely grate the Parmesan-style cheese and sprinkle over the dish. Return to the oven, uncovered, for a further 10 minutes. Serve.

TIP: Feta cheese also works well in this gratin. Replace the 25g vegetarian Parmesan-style cheese with 55g feta cheese. Use less salt in the sauce, as feta is a saltier cheese.

VEGETABLE SHEPHERD'S PIE
WITH SWEET POTATO MASH

We introduced this shepherd's pie to the deli, with sweet potato instead of potato mash, and it has become very popular. The orange colour of the sweet potato is a surprise alright, but it's cheering on a chilly night, and its mellow sugars complement the protein hit of the lentils well.

SERVES 6

FOR THE PIE:
UNREFINED SUNFLOWER OIL
1 ONION, FINELY DICED
1 SMALL LEEK
2 STICKS OF CELERY, FINELY DICED
1 CARROT, FINELY DICED
1 PARSNIP, FINELY DICED
1/2 COURGETTE, FINELY DICED
200 G (1/2 TIN) CHOPPED TOMATOES
55 G PUY OR GREEN LENTILS
175 G RED LENTILS
SEA SALT
2 TSP FRESH THYME
SOYA SAUCE

FOR THE MASH TOPPING:
4 SWEET POTATOES, APPROX. 900 G
2 OR 3 POTATOES, APPROX. 450 G
SEA SALT
BUTTER
2 TSP FRESH PARSLEY, FINELY CHOPPED

1 Heat 1 tbsp sunflower oil in a pot and sauté the onion for 2 minutes. Wash the leek well and slice both white and green parts thinly. Sauté with the onion for another 2 minutes. Add the celery, carrot, parsnip, courgette, tomatoes and a pinch of sea salt. Wash the puy lentils and stir into the vegetables. Wash the red lentils and lay them on top of the vegetables. It's best to keep the red lentils from the bottom of the pot when first cooking as they might stick to the bottom. Sprinkle with the chopped fresh thyme.

2 Cover with water to 2 cm above the red lentils and vegetables. Bring to a boil, cover tightly, lower the heat and simmer for 30 minutes.

3 Preheat the oven to Gas 5/190°C/375°F.

4 Peel and chop the sweet potatoes and potatoes and place in a pot with a pinch of salt. Cover with water and bring to a boil. Cover, lower the heat and simmer until the potatoes are tender, approx. 15 minutes. Mash well. Stir in a tablespoon of butter and the fresh parsley. Stir well until smooth. Season with sea salt.

5 When the lentils and vegetables are cooked, season with soya sauce to taste. Place in a 23 cm round x 5 cm deep ovenproof dish, Spread the mashed sweet potato topping over the lentil and vegetables and run a fork over it to make a ridged pattern. Bake for 20–30 minutes until the topping is beginning to brown and the centre of the pie is hot.

TIP: Other vegetables like turnip, daikon and butternut squash are also lovely in this dish.

LASAGNE

Lasagne is a perennial favourite. It's perfect for making at home on the weekend for a busy week ahead, and because I use lasagne sheets straight from the packet without pre-cooking, it's fairly hassle-free. The long cooking time is enough to cook the lasagne sheets through. There is a bit of preparation and assembly with lasagnes, so you might double the recipe, eat one and freeze one.

To make the lasagne sauce, place the flour in a separate pot and toast for a few minutes over a medium heat. Warm the milk. Pour it gradually onto the flour and whisk continuously to prevent lumps from forming. Add the bay leaf and a pinch of salt and on a medium heat and continue whisking until the sauce begins to bubble. Lower the heat and cook the sauce for 2 minutes. When the sauce has become thickened and creamy, remove from the heat. Stir in 55 g of the grated cheddar cheese. Check the seasoning.

Layer your ingredients as follows in a medium square or rectangular ovenproof dish (I used a pan that was 25 x 17 cm and 5cm deep). Spoon 4 tbsp sauce into the dish and spread out to the edges of the dish. Lay 3 sheets of lasagne on top. Spread half of the vegetable filling on top. Drop 4 tbsp of the sauce on top of the filling. Sprinkle over half of the grated cheddar. Lay 3 sheets of lasagne on top. Spread the rest of the filling on top of the lasagne sheets. Drop 4 tbsp sauce on top of the filling. Sprinkle over more of the cheddar. Lay the last 3 lasagne sheets on top. Pour the rest of the sauce on top. Sprinkle the last 25 g of cheddar cheese over the top. Finely grate the Parmesan-style cheese, and sprinkle it over the top of the lasagne. Place in the centre of the preheated oven for 50 minutes to 1 hour until the lasagne is bubbling and golden.

BUTTERNUT SQUASH LASAGNE WITH SAGE AND WALNUTS

SERVES 6
EXTRA VIRGIN OLIVE OIL
SEA SALT
1 LARGE BUTTERNUT SQUASH
1 ONION, FINELY DICED
6 SAGE LEAVES, FINELY CHOPPED
55 G TOASTED WALNUTS
COARSELY GROUND BLACK PEPPER
175 G VEGETARIAN CHEDDAR CHEESE, GRATED

9 SHEETS WHOLEMEAL SPELT LASAGNE
VEGETARIAN PARMESAN-STYLE CHEESE

FOR THE SAUCE:
70 G WHITE SPELT OR WHITE FLOUR
1 L MILK
1 BAY LEAF
SEA SALT

1 Preheat oven to Gas 7/220°C/425°F.

2 Peel the butternut squash and remove the seeds. Chop into 2 cm cubes and place onto a baking tray. Toss in 2 tbsp olive oil and a good pinch of sea salt. Place on the top shelf of the hot oven for 45 minutes until the butternut squash is cooked and brown around the edges.

3 Heat 1 tbsp olive oil in a pot. Sauté the onion over a medium heat until the onion is soft but not brown. Add the roasted butternut squash to the onions along with the fresh sage. Chop the walnuts and add to the pot. Season with salt and pepper. Set aside.

4 Lower the oven temperature to Gas 4/180°C/350°F.

5 Make the sauce, assemble the lasagne and bake.

6 Serve this lasagne with one of the slaws (p. 18–19) and a bean salad (p. 7), or for cooler weather, the French beans with Parmesan (p. 142).

VEGETABLE LASAGNE

SERVES 6
EXTRA VIRGIN OLIVE OIL
1 ONION, FINELY CHOPPED
1 STICK OF CELERY, FINELY DICED
2 CLOVES GARLIC, MINCED
1 CARROT, FINELY DICED
1 SMALL COURGETTE, FINELY DICED
400 G TIN CHOPPED TOMATOES
1 TSP ITALIAN DRIED HERBS (OR A MIX OF DRIED OREGANO AND DRIED BASIL)
SEA SALT
150 G ADUKI BEANS OR GREEN LENTILS, COOKED

FOR THE WHITE SAUCE:
55 G WHITE SPELT (OR PLAIN WHITE) FLOUR
750 ML MILK
2 BAY LEAVES
175 G VEGETARIAN CHEDDAR CHEESE

15 G VEGETARIAN PARMESAN-STYLE CHEESE
9 SHEETS WHOLEMEAL SPELT LASAGNE

1 Preheat oven to Gas 4/180°C/350°F.

2 Heat 2 tbsp olive oil in a pot and sauté the onion for 2 minutes. Add the celery and garlic and cook for a minute more. Remove from the heat and add the carrot, courgette, tomatoes, herbs and a good pinch of salt. Pour in 225 ml water. Cover and bring to a boil, then lower the heat and simmer for 20 minutes. Stir a few times to ensure the vegetables don't stick to the pot. Add the aduki beans and mix well.

3 Heat the oven. Check the seasoning of the cooked filling, make the sauce and begin assembling the lasagne. I used a 25 x 17 cm by 5 cm deep ovenproof dish.

4 Place in the centre of the preheated oven and bake for 1 hour until the lasagne is bubbling.

STIR-FRY WITH NOODLES AND AMAI SAUCE

This is a very versatile dish that can include cauliflower florets, peas, corn, bean sprouts or mushrooms.

SERVES 6
1 PACKAGE EGG NOODLES
2 CARROTS, SLICED INTO 5CM JULIENNE
10 CM PIECE DAIKON, PEELED AND SLICED INTO 5 CM JULIENNE
1 HEAD BROCCOLI, DIVIDED INTO BITE-SIZED FLORETS
UNREFINED SUNFLOWER, SESAME OR RAPESEED OIL
1¹/₂ MEDIUM ONIONS, HALVED AND SLICED INTO HALF MOONS
1 COURGETTE, HALVED AND SLICED ON THE DIAGONAL
¹/₂ RED PEPPER, SLICED INTO THIN STRIPS
3 SCALLIONS, SLICED INTO THIN ROUNDS
FRESH PARSLEY, CHOPPED, TO GARNISH

FOR THE AMAI SAUCE:
1 TBSP RICE VINEGAR
1¹/₂ TBSP TOMATO PUREE
1 TBSP AGAVE SYRUP
2 TSP TAMARIND
2 TBSP SOYA SAUCE

1 Place the ingredients for the amai sauce into the bowl of a food processor and blend until smooth.

2 Boil a large pot of water and cook the noodles for 3 minutes, (al dente). Rinse in plenty of cold water, drain and set aside.

3 Place the prepared carrots, daikon and broccoli florets into a pot with ½ cm water. Place a tight lid on top, bring to a boil, lower the heat and cook the vegetables for 2 minutes. Remove the lid and set aside.

4 Heat 2 tbsp unrefined oil in a pan or wok over a medium heat. Sauté the onions for 2 minutes. Add the carrots, daikon, broccoli, courgette and red pepper. Add the scallions to the pan. If there is any juice left from steaming the vegetables, add it to the pan. Sauté for 3–4 minutes until the vegetables are cooked. Add the cooked noodles and toss together. Pour the amai sauce over the vegetables and noodles and toss together until all the vegetables and noodles are mixed well. Check the seasoning and add extra soya sauce if needed. Sprinkle with chopped fresh parsley and serve.

5 Serve with baked or pan-fried tofu, page 140.

TIP: Rice noodles, soba noodles or wheat noodles also work well with this dish.

TIP: The absolutely finger-licking amai sauce keeps well in the fridge for up to 3 weeks.

VEGETABLE WELLINGTON WITH ONION GRAVY

This recipe came about when I was asked for a centrepiece dish for a vegetarian Christmas table for the Afternoon Show.

SERVES 4 TO 6

60 G BROWN BASMATI RICE

PINCH SAFFRON OR TURMERIC

1 TSP LEMON ZEST (ABOUT HALF A LEMON)

1/2 CINNAMON STICK

1 SMALL ONION, HALVED AND THINLY SLICED

1 BAY LEAF

2 CLOVES

2 GREEN CARDAMOM PODS

3 LARGE PORTOBELLO MUSHROOMS

300 G BUTTERNUT SQUASH, DICED INTO 2 CM CUBES

SUNFLOWER MARGARINE

SUNFLOWER OIL

1 TBSP PARSLEY, FINELY CHOPPED

1 TBSP THYME LEAVES, FINELY CHOPPED

2 FREE RANGE EGGS, HARD BOILED AND ROUGHLY CHOPPED

SEA SALT AND FRESH GROUND BLACK PEPPER

330 G PUFF PASTRY

1 FREE RANGE EGG, BEATEN

FOR THE ONION GRAVY:

1 MEDIUM ONION, FINELY DICED

2 TSP THYME LEAVES, FINELY CHOPPED

250 ML VEGETABLE STOCK

SOY SAUCE TO TASTE

2 TSP ARROWROOT, KUZU OR CORNFLOUR TO THICKEN

1 Preheat oven to Gas 7/220°C/425°F.

2 Wash the rice. Using a pot with a tight lid and over a medium heat, melt 2 tsp margarine, and 2 tsp oil. Sauté the onion until soft. Add the cinnamon stick, bay leaf, cloves, cardamom pods, and the pinch of saffron. Add the rice, 100 ml water and a pinch of salt. Bring to a boil, lower the heat, cover tightly and simmer on a low heat for 45 minutes.

3 Meanwhile, place the butternut squash onto a baking tray and toss in a little oil and a pinch of salt. Place on the top shelf of a hot oven to roast for about 15 minutes. Remove the stalks from the mushrooms. Wipe the mushroom caps clean. Place on another baking tray and toss in a little oil and a pinch of salt and sprinkle over half the thyme leaves. Dice the mushroom stalks and add to the baking tray. Toss in the sunflower oil and a little salt. Place in the hot oven to roast until tender, about 15 minutes.

4 Lower the oven temperature to Gas 6/200°C/400°F.

Fluff up the rice and remove the cinnamon stick, bay leaf, cardamom pods and cloves. Place in a large bowl along with the roasted butternut squash, parsley, the remaining thyme leaves, lemon zest, mushroom stalks and hard- boiled eggs. Stir and season with salt and pepper.

5 Lightly grease a baking tray. To assemble the Wellington, lightly flour a work surface and roll out the puff pastry to 1/2 cm thick. Cut a rectangle of pastry 20 x 30 cm. Lay the mushrooms down the middle of the rectangle of pastry. Place the rice mixture on top. Bring the sides of the pastry up together and pinch together to seal. With the remaining pastry, cut out some leaf shapes to decorate the pie. Lift onto the oiled baking tray. Brush the surface with beaten egg, add decorations and brush decorations. Place in the centre of the oven for 30 minutes until golden.

6 To make the gravy, warm a dessertspoon of oil in a pot and sauté the onion and thyme until the onion is soft but not brown. Add the vegetable stock. Blend the arrowroot/cornflour/kuzu into a little cold water and add to the pot. Bring to a boil, lower the heat and simmer until the gravy thickens. Season to taste with soy sauce for richness.

TIP: This dish can be made as early as 8 hours in advance. Follow the recipe above, stopping before the egg-wash stage. Cover with cling film and refrigerate. When ready to bake, heat the oven, remove the cling film, brush with beaten egg. Place in the centre of the oven for 30 minutes until golden.

BUTTERNUT SQUASH, SPINACH AND BUTTER BEAN GRATIN

This is an eye-catching centrepiece dish, with layers of vibrant colours from the butternut squash, spinach and feta. Serve this gratin with the barley or rice salad or with one of the simpler cooked grains to help soak up the tasty juices.

SERVES 6 TO 8

1 LARGE BUTTERNUT SQUASH
500 G SPINACH LEAVES (OR 350 G FROZEN SPINACH LEAVES)
1 ONION, HALVED AND THINLY SLICED
2 CLOVES GARLIC
EXTRA VIRGIN OLIVE OIL
400 G TIN OF BUTTER BEANS (OR 350 G FRESHLY COOKED BUTTER BEANS)
100 G FETA CHEESE
200 ML FRESH CREAM
100 G GRATED VEGETARIAN CHEDDAR CHEESE
50 G BREADCRUMBS
6 SAGE LEAVES
SEA SALT
BLACK PEPPER

1 Preheat oven to Gas 6/200°C/400°F.

2 Wash the spinach leaves and remove the thick stems. Place in a pot with 2 tbsp water and allow to wilt. Drain the spinach in a colander. If using frozen spinach, defrost and drain in a colander also. Fry the onion gently in some olive oil along with the garlic until soft. Chop the wilted and drained spinach leaves. Add to the pan and fry for a few minutes more. Season lightly. Set aside. Peel the butternut squash and remove the seeds. Halve lengthwise and slice thinly into ½ cm slices. Rinse and drain the beans. Use a 25 x 18 cm ovenproof dish at least 5 cm deep. Layer half of the sliced butternut squash in the dish, seasoning lightly as you go. Spread the spinach mix evenly over the squash and crumble the feta cheese on top. Place the butter beans on top of the spinach and feta. Lay the remaining sliced butternut squash on top, seasoning lightly as you go. Press down with your hands. Pour the cream over, ensuring that it trickles down through the layers. Cover with tin foil and place on the top shelf of the preheated oven for 30 minutes or until the squash is soft. Remove the foil and sprinkle with the grated cheddar cheese.

3 Finely chop the sage and mix with the breadcrumbs. Sprinkle on top of dish. Place back into the oven for a further 15 minutes until the dish is golden brown and cooked through. Allow to rest out of the oven for 5–10 minutes before serving.

TIP: This can be made without the cream if you prefer, but I love the richness it brings to the dish.

FILO PIES

Filo pastry strikes fear in the hearts of even accomplished of bakers, but as ready-made filo can be purchased frozen, there's really no need to worry, particularly as it's well floured and easy to handle (gently) as soon as it's thawed. You can find filo in most supermarkets, but the best quality filo comes from the Asian stores. Interestingly enough, they stock Greek brands, which have no additives and handle better.

Both filo pies here are cut before they are cooked because the filo becomes crisp and delicate when baked, and crumbles too much to be cut after it comes out of the oven. The lightness of the pastry really shows off the quality of the fresh veg and cheese in these recipes, so do use the best you can.

SPANAKOPITA

My sister-in-law, Kathy, gave me this recipe, and it was given to her by her Greek mother-in-law. It is a light dish, with a crisp filo topping and lovely seasoning of fresh dill.

SERVES 6
1 KG SPINACH LEAVES
2 MEDIUM LEEKS
EXTRA VIRGIN OLIVE OIL
SEA SALT
4 FREE RANGE EGGS
450 G FETA CHEESE
2 TBSP CHOPPED FRESH DILL
1 UNWAXED LEMON
COARSELY GROUND BLACK PEPPER
6 SHEETS FILO PASTRY

1 Preheat oven to Gas 4/180°C/350°F.

2 Wash the spinach well. Keep the spinach stalks if they are not too tough. Place in a pot of boiling water to wilt for about 5 minutes. Drain in a colander and allow to cool slightly, to make it easier to handle.

3 Heat 3 tbsp olive oil in a deep pan. Slice the leeks in half lengthwise and wash well. Slice thinly and cook over a low heat so that the leek cooks but doesn't brown. After 5 minutes, chop the spinach and add to the pan. Season with a pinch of salt. Cook until the spinach and leeks are tender. Set aside to cool.

4 Whisk the eggs. Add to the spinach and leeks along with the dill and the grated rind of half the lemon. Crumble the feta and add to the mix. Season with salt and pepper, but keep in mind that the feta cheese is salty.

5 Lay the filo sheets out on a flat surface. Oil a 30 x 25 cm by 5 cm deep ovenproof dish. Lay one sheet of filo lengthwise in the dish allowing the edges to overlap the sides of the dish. Oil the sheet of filo lightly. Lay a second sheet on top of the first. Oil this sheet lightly. Repeat this two more times, allowing each sheet to overlap the sides, and oiling lightly each time. Pour the spinach and feta mix into the dish. Fold the last two sheets of filo pastry in half and place on top of the spinach mix. Oil the layers lightly. Fold over the overlapping layers of filo on top of the pie. Oil the top lightly and, using a sharp knife, cut the pie into triangular portions. Bake in the centre of the preheated oven for 25 minutes until golden and the centre is set.

6 Serve with quinoa taboulleh (p. 23).

COURGETTE AND GOAT'S CHEESE PIE

This is a light pie with lovely subtle flavours, perfect for using up a summer glut of courgettes. It also showcases one of my favourite cheeses, Ryefield goat log from Co. Tyrone, though many good Irish cheeses can fit the bill here.

SERVES 6 TO 8
EXTRA VIRGIN OLIVE OIL
2 ONIONS
1 CLOVE GARLIC, MINCED
3 COURGETTES, ABOUT 700 G
SEA SALT
COARSELY GROUND BLACK PEPPER
4 FREE RANGE EGGS
2 TBSP FRESH BASIL, FINELY CHOPPED
280 G GOAT'S CHEESE
5 SHEETS FILO PASTRY

1 Preheat oven to Gas 4/180°C/350°F.

2 Heat a deep pan over a medium heat. Quarter the onions and slice thinly. Warm 3 tbsp olive oil in the pan and add the onion and sauté for 3 minutes. Do not let the onion brown, just soften. Coarsely grate the courgette and add to the pan with the garlic. Cook until the courgette and the onion are soft. Season with salt and pepper and set aside to cool.

3 Heat the oven. Oil a 27 cm flan dish. A glass or ceramic dish works best. Whisk the eggs and add to the vegetables along with the fresh basil. If the goat's cheese has rind, remove it and crumble the cheese into the vegetable and egg mix. Season.

4 Lay the sheets of filo pastry onto a flat surface. Place one sheet into the flan dish, allowing the edges spill over the edge. Oil the pastry lightly. Lay a second sheet in the flan dish in the opposite direction, again allowing the pastry to spill over the edge of the dish. Oil lightly. Repeat with another 2 sheets of pastry. Pour the filling into the filo-lined flan dish. Smooth it out evenly. Cut the last sheet of filo in half and place on top of the filling and oil lightly. Fold over the sides of the pastry on to the top of the pie, until a nice round shape forms. The pastry will be uneven on the top but it will look good once baked.

5 Lightly oil the pie, and with a large, sharp knife, cut into 6 or 8 pieces. Place in the centre of the preheated oven for 30 minutes until the pie is golden brown and the centre is set.

TIP: This pie can be served hot or cold. It travels well, so it's a lovely picnic dish.

It works with ratatouille vegetables (p. 149) tossed with chickpeas or cannellini beans, the chickpea, red onion and chilli salad (p. 9) or the pasta salad with rocket (p. 6). It is light enough to serve 12 as a starter with some lightly dressed leaves.

HALLOUMI AND VEGETABLE KEBABS

These kebabs can be cooked on the barbeque or a pan, and look fantastic served with carrot and daikon salad, p. 2.

SERVES 6
500 G HALLOUMI CHEESE
9 BABY POTATOES
2 RED PEPPERS
2 RED ONIONS

FOR THE MARINADE:
75 ML EXTRA VIRGIN OLIVE OIL
2 CLOVES GARLIC, CHOPPED

2 TSP ROSEMARY
2 TSP MINT
2 TSP PARSLEY
2 TSP THYME
JUICE OF 1 LIME
SEA SALT
COARSE GROUND BLACK PEPPER

6 WOODEN SKEWERS

1 Blend all of the marinade ingredients in a food processor or with a hand blender. Pour into a large bowl.

2 Cook the potatoes in salted water until tender but not mushy, approx. 10 minutes. Slice the cooked potatoes in half. Chop the halloumi into approx. 2½ cm cubes. Remove the seeds from the peppers and chop into approx. 2½ cm pieces. Add the potatoes, halloumi and peppers to the marinade and toss well. Cut the red onions into quarters. Add to the marinade. Toss carefully to ensure that the onion quarters don't separate into smaller pieces. Set aside in the fridge overnight or for at least 6 hours.

3 If using a barbeque, get it going and allow it to heat up. Soak the skewers in water for 30 minutes so that they don't burn. When you're ready to cook the kebabs, skewer 2 pieces of red onion, 2 pieces red pepper, 3 pieces potato and 4 cubes halloumi, alternating ingredients as you go. Set aside and repeat with the other 5 skewers.

4 If using a pan, heat it over a medium heat. Place 3 skewers onto the dry pan at a time; you do not need to oil the pan as there is enough oil in the marinade. As the vegetables and halloumi cheese brown, turn the kebabs over until each side has cooked.

5 If using a barbeque, place the skewers onto the hot barbeque. Halloumi cheese grills very well on the barbeque, but should be watched closely to ensure that it doesn't burn. Turn the kebabs to grill each side evenly.

6 Drizzle the kebabs with a little of the marinade before serving, and serve on quinoa (p. 129) or bulgur (p. 124) with yoghurt and mint sauce (p. 107) on the side.

HERBED ROULADE WITH A ROASTED TOMATO AND FRESH BASIL SAUCE

A roulade is rolled up like a Swiss roll, but don't let that put you off. Unlike the Swiss roll, which uses a light sponge that can split and fall apart, a roulade base is more like a frittata. It's firm and easy to work with, even for a first-timer.

Read the method in full before you start. When rolling up the roulade, be focused and just go for it – like flipping pancakes, it can't be done in half measures. Firmness rather than the delicate touch is what you need.

The nice thing about this dish is it can be prepared 4–5 hours in advance of eating so you don't have to do it as your guests are arriving.

SERVES 6

FOR THE ROULADE BASE:
5 FREE RANGE EGGS
300 ML MILK
55 G BUTTER, OR SUNFLOWER MARGARINE
55 G WHITE SPELT FLOUR OR PLAIN FLOUR
15 G FRESH DILL
2 TSP FLAT LEAF PARSLEY
70 G VEGETARIAN PARMESAN-STYLE CHEESE

FOR THE ROULADE FILLING:
1 KG SPINACH LEAVES
2 TBSP EXTRA VIRGIN OLIVE OIL
1/2 ONION, FINELY CHOPPED
1 TBSP TOASTED PINE NUTS (OPTIONAL)
175 G SOFT GOAT'S CHEESE
115 G RICOTTA CHEESE
SEA SALT
FRESHLY GROUND BLACK PEPPER

FOR THE SAUCE:
1 KG TOMATOES
4 TBSP EXTRA VIRGIN OLIVE OIL
2 CLOVES GARLIC
15 G FRESH BASIL
SEA SALT
COARSELY GROUND BLACK PEPPER

1 Preheat oven to Gas 7/220°C/425°F.

2 To make the tomato sauce, wash and dry the tomatoes, and place the whole tomatoes in an oven proof dish, along with the cloves of garlic. Put in a preheated oven on the top shelf. Roast for 20 minutes. Give the dish a shake half way through roasting to turn the tomatoes. Allow the tomatoes and garlic cloves to cool slightly and remove the skins – they should slip off easily.

Place the tomatoes and garlic in a food processor, or use a hand blender, along with the fresh basil and blend. Strain through a sieve. Season to taste with sea salt and pepper. Set aside.

3 To make the roulade base, lower the oven temperature to Gas 6/200°C/400°F.

4 Line a 37 x 25 cm baking tin with greaseproof paper. Oil and flour the lined tin lightly, shaking off any excess flour.

5 Separate the yolks and egg whites; whisk the yolks lightly and set both aside.

6 Warm the milk. In a pot melt the butter or margarine, add the flour. Stirring constantly, cook for 1–2 minutes over a medium heat. Whisk in the warm milk, and cook for 3 minutes, continuing to stir constantly to avoid lumps.

7 Gradually whisk some of the hot mixture into the egg yolks and then return to the pot to continue cooking the roux until thickened and smooth. Season with sea salt. Whisk in the finely chopped herbs and half of the vegetarian Parmesan-style cheese. Whisk the egg whites until stiff. With a metal spoon, stir a third of the egg whites into the roux, gently fold in the rest of the egg whites.

8 Pour the mixture onto the prepared baking tin, spreading it into all the corners.

9 Bake in the centre of the oven until risen and golden, about 15 minutes. Place on a cooling tray.

10 While the base is in the oven, make the filling. Wash and remove the stems from the spinach leaves. Wilt the spinach in a covered pot with 2 tbsp water until soft. Drain in a colander. Heat the olive oil in a pan and sauté the onion until soft but not browned. Squeeze the excess liquid from the spinach by pressing it into the colander, chop finely and add to the pan. Cook for a few minutes. Season with salt.

11 Place the soft goat's cheese and ricotta cheese into a bowl and with a little sea salt and pepper. Whisk together.

12 Lay a sheet of greaseproof paper onto a flat surface and sprinkle with the remaining vegetarian Parmesan-style cheese. Turn the baked roulade base onto the greaseproof paper and cheese. Gently peel off the greaseproof paper on which the base was baked. Don't worry if the base 'falls' when you take it out of the hot oven – it's a dense mixture and this is to be expected. Spread the goat's cheese and ricotta mixture over the base, and cover it with the spinach mixture. If using pine nuts, sprinkle over the spinach mixture. Starting with the short end, roll up the roulade using the greaseproof paper to help. Press firmly as you roll. Place on a lightly oiled baking tin. Cover with foil and bake until the roulade is heated through, about 25 minutes.

13 Warm the tomato sauce.

14 To serve, ladle tomato sauce onto a plate and place a slice of roulade on the sauce.

TIP: The sauce can be made in advance, and the roulade itself can be prepared for baking a few hours ahead of time, wrapped in cling film and refrigerated. When ready to bake, unwrap and bake as above.

TIP: If you don't have ricotta cheese, whip 125 ml fresh cream until stiff and fold the goat's cheese into it. This will give the spanakopita the moisture it needs.

FRITTATA

This is a great way to eat up leftover boiled potatoes and steamed or roasted vegetables. Every time you make it, it's going to taste a little different, as it will depend on which vegetables are left over, what herbs you have around and what kind of cheese you use.

SERVES 6 TO 8
1 ONION, DICED
4 BOILED POTATOES, PEELED AND DICED
1 BOWL OF STEAMED OR LEFTOVER ROASTED VEGETABLES
4 LARGE FREE RANGE EGGS
2 TSP HERBS (PARSLEY, OREGANO, CHIVES, BASIL) CHOPPED FINELY
SMALL HANDFUL CHEESE
EXTRA VIRGIN OLIVE OIL
SEA SALT
PEPPER

1 Heat the frying pan over a medium heat. Add a tablespoon of olive oil and fry the onion gently until soft but not brown. Add the diced cooked potato and fry until the potato becomes brown at the edges. Add the vegetables and season with salt and pepper and stir in any herbs at this stage.

2 Beat the eggs. Lower the heat and pour the eggs over the potato and vegetables mixture. Stir to combine the egg and vegetables. Press down with the back of a wooden spoon and allow the dish to set. Keep the heat low. When the dish is almost set, sprinkle with grated or crumbled cheese. Place under the grill to set and brown the top.

3 Slide a spatula around the edges of the frittata to help to free it from the pan. Slide the finished frittata onto a plate and slice into wedges.

4 Serve with French beans with Parmesan (p. 142).

TIP: If you don't have any leftover cooked vegetables, double the amount of potatoes and use the same method to make a Spanish tortilla, a thick omelette made from onion and potato. Both dishes are also very good cold, and ideal for a picnic or in a lunch box.

STUFFED TOMATOES WITH YOGHURT AND MINT SAUCE

If you can get your hands on some homegrown tomatoes between the months of July and November, make this dish. Delicious.

SERVES 6

FOR THE STUFFED TOMATOES:
150 G BROWN BASMATI RICE
VEGETABLE STOCK CUBE
175 ML WATER
6 BEEF TOMATOES, RIPE BUT FIRM
EXTRA VIRGIN OLIVE OIL
1 CLOVE GARLIC, MINCED
1 ONION, FINELY CHOPPED
25 G TOASTED PINE NUTS
1 TBSP FRESH MINT, FINELY CHOPPED
1 TBSP FRESH PARSLEY, FINELY CHOPPED
25 G GRATED VEGETARIAN PARMESAN-STYLE CHEESE
SEA SALT
COARSELY GROUND BLACK PEPPER

FOR THE YOGHURT AND MINT SAUCE:
250G THICK NATURAL YOGHURT
2 TSP FRESH MINT, FINELY CHOPPED
SEA SALT

1 Wash the rice and place in a pot with a tight lid. Crumble in the stock cube and pour in 225 ml water. Bring to a boil, lower the heat and cover. Simmer for 45 minutes. Slice the tops off of the tomatoes and save them. Scoop out the pulp. Chop and save the juices.

2 Preheat the oven to Gas 4/180°C/350°F.

3 Heat 1 tbsp olive oil in a pan, add the onion and garlic and cook over a medium heat until the onion is soft. Add the tomato and juices and a pinch of sea salt and cook until the juices have reduced. Check the seasoning. Fluff up the cooked rice and add the mint, parsley, pine nuts, tomato, onion, and cheese. Season with salt and pepper. Using a spoon, stuff the tomatoes with the filling. Leave a little room to allow the rice to expand. Place the lids on top and drizzle with olive oil. Place in an ovenproof dish and bake for 50 minutes to 1 hour.

4 Meanwhile, make the dressing by combining the yoghurt and mint together in a bowl and seasoning with sea salt. Serve on the side of the stuffed tomatoes.

TARTS

Tarts are always an attractive way to present your best, tastiest vegetables, and they can be cut and served at the table. These tarts all freeze well, and are good either hot or cold. If you prefer a lighter tart, you can replace any cream in the following recipes with milk.

The basic pastry is made as follows. First, preheat your oven to Gas 5/190°C/375°F. Lightly oil a 28 cm tart tin. To make the tart base, place the flour in a large mixing bowl. Add a pinch of salt. Rub in the butter until the mixture resembles breadcrumbs. Add 20 ml cold water, and bring together the mix into a soft ball of dough with your fingers. Wrap in some cling film and place in the fridge to rest for 30 minutes.

Turn out the rested dough onto a lightly floured surface. Flour the rolling pin to prevent the dough from sticking. Roll out the dough to fit the tart tin, remembering it needs to be larger than the base to allow for the depth of the tin. Bring the dough up the sides of the tin. Gently press the dough into the sides and base of the tin. Trim around the edge of the tin. With floured forefingers press the dough into the sides of the pastry to create a ridged design. This will help to give the pastry some height, to allow for a little shrinkage during baking. Prick the base with a fork and place in a preheated oven to bake for 20 minutes. The base should be lightly golden.

VEGAN SUMMER TART

This is the vegan version – and it's so tasty that it will be enjoyed by everyone, not just vegans. Serve it first, then tell them it's tofu. Maybe you should even try this before the vegetarian version, just for something different.

SERVES 6 TO 8

FOR THE BASE:
175 G FINE WHOLEMEAL SPELT FLOUR
SEA SALT
85 G SUNFLOWER MARGARINE

FOR THE FILLING:
EXTRA VIRGIN OLIVE OIL
1 SMALL LEEK
1 SMALL CARROT
1 SMALL COURGETTE
1 LARGE CLOVE GARLIC, MINCED
SEA SALT
2 TSP FRESH THYME, FINELY CHOPPED
2 TSP FRESH PARSLEY, FINELY CHOPPED
2 CUBES FRESH TOFU
SOY SAUCE
COARSELY GROUND BLACK PEPPER

1 Preheat oven to Gas 5/190°C/375°F. Prepare and pre-bake the pastry and cut and cook the vegetables as above.

2 Place the tofu in a food processor or use a hand blender. Add 1 tbsp soya sauce and 2 tbsp water. Blend until smooth. Stir ⅔ of the blended tofu into the vegetables and mix well. Pour onto the pre-baked tart base. Spread out evenly. Pour the rest of the blended tofu on top and spread out evenly.

3 Place in the centre of the oven and bake for a further 25 minutes until the tart has set and is golden brown. Serve hot or cold.

SWISS CHARD TART WITH FETA AND FRESH DILL

This tart was originally made with spinach leaves, but once I started growing my own rainbow chard, I found that the colourful stems make it a very attractive dish.

SERVES 6 TO 8

FOR THE BASE:
175 G FINE WHOLEMEAL SPELT FLOUR
SEA SALT
85 G SUNFLOWER MARGARINE OR BUTTER

FOR THE FILLING:
350 G SWISS CHARD
1 MEDIUM ONION
1 LARGE CLOVE OF GARLIC
EXTRA VIRGIN OLIVE OIL
SEA SALT
COARSE GROUND BLACK PEPPER
4 FREE RANGE EGGS PLUS 2 EGG YOLKS
150 ML FRESH CREAM
100 ML MILK
1 TBSP FRESH DILL, FINELY CHOPPED
120 G FETA CHEESE

1 Preheat oven to Gas 5/190°C/375°F.

2 Prepare and pre-bake the pastry base as p. 110.

3 Bring a large pot of water to the boil. Wash the chard leaves and stalks and blanch in the boiling water for 5 minutes. If the leaves are young this should only take 2–3 minutes. Drain in a colander.

4 Heat 2 tbsp olive oil in a deep pan. Dice the onion and sauté until soft, add the garlic and sauté for a further 2 minutes. Chop the stalks and leaves of the wilted chard into 6 mm pieces. Add to the softened onion and sauté until the stalks are tender, about 10 minutes. Season with salt and pepper. Place onto the baked tart base. Crumble the feta roughly over the vegetables. Sprinkle the fresh dill over the feta.

5 Whisk the eggs, cream and milk together. Season with just a little salt, as feta is a salty cheese. Pour over the chard mix, helping it to move down through the vegetables with a fork.

6 Place in the centre of the preheated oven and bake for 30 minutes until the tart has set and it is golden brown.

7 Serve hot or cold.

TIP: If using spinach leaves in this tart, do not use baby spinach as they are too tender. Follow the recipe as above.

SUMMER LEEK TART

The flavours of the three vegetables in this picnic staple really complement each other.

SERVES 6 TO 8

FOR THE BASE:
175 G FINE WHOLEMEAL SPELT FLOUR
SEA SALT
85 G SUNFLOWER MARGARINE OR BUTTER

FOR THE FILLING:
EXTRA VIRGIN OLIVE OIL
1 SMALL LEEK
1 MEDIUM CARROT
1 MEDIUM COURGETTE
1 LARGE CLOVE GARLIC, MINCED
SEA SALT
2 TSP FRESH THYME, FINELY CHOPPED
2 TSP FRESH PARSLEY, FINELY CHOPPED
4 FREE RANGE EGGS PLUS 2 FREE RANGE EGG YOLKS
150 ML FRESH CREAM
100 ML MILK
25 G VEGETARIAN PARMESAN-STYLE CHEESE
COARSELY GROUND BLACK PEPPER

1 Preheat oven to Gas 5/190°C/375°F and prepare and pre-bake the pastry as page 108.

2 Make the filling. Slice the leek in half lengthwise and wash well. Let the water run between the layers as they can hold sand. Cut into 4 cm pieces and slice into thin julienne. Slice the carrot and courgette into thin julienne, 4 cm inches in length. Heat 3 tbsp olive oil in a pan over a medium heat. Add the leek and cook slowly for 3 minutes. Add the garlic, carrots, courgettes, thyme and a pinch of salt and cook for a further 5 minutes until the vegetables are tender. Lower the heat if the vegetables are browning too quickly. Stir in the parsley and season with salt and pepper. Finely grate the cheese and sprinkle ⅓ over the baked tart base. Place the vegetables evenly onto the base.

3 Whisk the eggs and egg yolks together and whisk in the cream and milk. Lightly season with salt. Pour the egg mix over the vegetables, moving down through the vegetables with the help of a fork. Sprinkle the rest of the cheese on top. Place in the centre of the preheated oven and bake for 30 minutes until the tart has set and it is golden brown.

4 Serve hot or cold.

TIP: A hard goat's cheese works just as well as the vegetarian Parmesan-style cheese; we particularly like Clonmore from Co. Cork.

TWO-POTATO THREE-CHEESE TART

This tart is a bit different, as it uses an oat-based pastry. It's perfect alongside a chunky soup for dinner, or with a side of broccoli with toasted hazelnuts, p. 132.

SERVES 6 TO 8

FOR THE OAT PASTRY BASE:
120 G JUMBO OAT FLAKES
120 G WHOLEMEAL SPELT FLOUR
120 G SUNFLOWER MARGARINE OR BUTTER
SEA SALT

FOR THE FILLING:
800 G WAXY POTATOES
450 G SWEET POTATOES
UNREFINED SUNFLOWER OIL
EXTRA VIRGIN OLIVE OIL
3 ONIONS, HALVED AND SLICED

2 CLOVES GARLIC, MINCED
SEA SALT
3 FREE RANGE EGGS
2 FREE RANGE EGG YOLKS
150 ML FRESH CREAM
50 ML OF MILK
100 G FETA CHEESE
125 G MATURE WHITE VEGETARIAN CHEDDAR
  CHEESE, GRATED
1 TBSP FRESH THYME, FINELY CHOPPED
1¹/₂ TBSP FRESH PARSLEY, FINELY CHOPPED
25 G VEGETARIAN PARMESAN-STYLE CHEESE

1 Place the flour, oat flakes, pinch of salt and margarine into a food processor. Pulse until the mix resembles breadcrumbs. With the motor running, add 30 ml cold water, gradually, until the dough comes together. Form the dough into a ball and roll in cling film and refrigerate for 30 minutes.

2 Preheat oven to Gas 5/190°C/375°F.

3 Make the filling. Peel the waxy potatoes and boil in salted until tender. Peel the sweet potatoes and boil in salted water for 10 minutes until tender and not mushy. Drain the potatoes and set aside to cool. Slice the cooked potatoes thinly.

4 Heat a pan over a medium heat and add 1 tbsp unrefined sunflower oil and 2 tbsp olive oil. Sauté the onions and garlic until soft. Season with sea salt and ½ tbsp fresh thyme.

5 After 30 minutes, take the dough out of the fridge. Roll out and line a 28 cm flan dish. Place in the preheated oven for 20 minutes until the base is firm to the touch.

6 Place the cooked onions onto the pre-baked flan base. Crumble the feta cheese on top. Layer half of the sliced waxy potatoes on top. Sprinkle with half of the grated vegetarian cheddar, the rest of the thyme and ½ tbsp parsley. Place the sliced sweet potatoes on top. Layer the rest of the waxy potatoes on top. Sprinkle the rest of the cheddar cheese, 1 tbsp chopped parsley and the vegetarian Parmesan-style cheese.

7 Whisk the eggs and the egg yolks together with the fresh cream and milk. Season with sea salt and pepper. Pour the egg and cream mix down through the potatoes. Move the potatoes gently to help the egg and cream mix to travel down through the tart. Bake for 40 minutes until set.

WINTER VEGETABLE PIE

Best made and enjoyed on one of those days you'd rather stay in with a good book and a glass of wine. It takes a little longer than some of the recipes, but what better way to spend a cold afternoon than in a warm kitchen?

SERVES 4 TO 6

FOR THE SHORTCRUST PASTRY:
100 G WHOLEMEAL SPELT FLOUR
100 G WHITE SPELT FLOUR
100 G SUNFLOWER MARGARINE
PINCH OF SEA SALT

FOR THE FILLING:
4 STICKS CELERY
4 CARROTS
2 PARSNIPS
1 TURNIP
150 G MUSHROOMS
2 LARGE CLOVES GARLIC, MINCED
1 TBSP MIXED FRESH HERBS, FINELY CHOPPED: PARSLEY, THYME AND OREGANO
EXTRA VIRGIN OLIVE OIL
1 FREE RANGE EGG, BEATEN

FOR THE ONION GRAVY:
1 ONION, FINELY DICED
250 ML VEGETABLE STOCK
30 G WHITE SPELT OR PLAIN FLOUR
1 TBSP SUNFLOWER MARGARINE
SOY SAUCE TO TASTE

1 Sift both flours into a large bowl. Add the salt and margarine. Rub the margarine into the flour with your fingertips until the mix resembles bread crumbs. Add 30 ml cold water and, using your fingertips, bring the mix together until a ball of dough forms. Wrap in cling film and refrigerate for at least 30 minutes.

2 Wash the celery and slice into pieces 2½ cm thick. Heat some olive oil in a large pot and add the celery and sauté for a few minutes. Wipe the mushrooms and add to the pot along with the garlic. Peel the carrots and parsnips, halve lengthwise, slice into 2½ cm pieces and add to the pot. Continue stirring the vegetables. Dice turnip into 2½ cm pieces and add to the vegetables. Add 1 or 2 cm of water and a pinch of salt. Bring to a boil, lower the heat, cover and simmer for 7 or 8 minutes. Stir in the herbs and season with pepper. Set aside to cool.

3 Make the gravy. Melt the butter in a pot and fry the onions over a low heat until soft. Add the flour and cook for 2 minutes. Remove from the heat and add the stock slowly, whisking constantly to avoid lumps. Return to the heat and bring to a boil, lower the heat and cook for 2 minutes. Season with soy sauce to make a rich sauce.

4 Preheat oven to Gas 4/180°C/350°F.

5 Using a 23 cm round baking dish or a 23 x 13 cm ovenproof dish, assemble the pie.

6 Stir the gravy into the vegetables. Season with soy sauce. Pour into the baking dish.

7 Roll out the pastry to ¼ cm thick. Cut to 2½ cm larger than the baking dish. Lay the pastry on top of the vegetables and gravy. Turn the edges under. Brush with beaten egg. If there is pastry left over, cut out some shapes and lay them on the pastry and brush with egg also. Prick the pastry twice with a fork. Bake in the preheated oven for 30 to 40 minutes until golden.

HOTPOTS

...is really your only man, and though many of the Blazing Salads hot dishes ...deli) fall into this category, these are the shining stars. They're winning ...be made in advance – indeed, the flavours improve if they're made the day ahead. Fragrant rice (p. 126) is a must with these dishes.

CHICKPEA, BUTTERNUT SQUASH AND SPINACH CURRY

The lovely creamy richness of this curry has always been a hit with teenagers in my house. Conveniently, it cooks quickly and can be doubled easily to feed a crowd.

SERVES 6

1 BUTTERNUT SQUASH, ABOUT 20 CM HIGH
200 G SPINACH LEAVES
UNREFINED SUNFLOWER OIL
1 TSP CUMIN SEEDS
2 TSP BROWN MUSTARD SEEDS
1 ONION, CHOPPED
2 LARGE CLOVES GARLIC, CHOPPED FINELY
1 GREEN CHILLI, DESEEDED AND CHOPPED FINELY
2¹/₂ CM PIECE FRESH GINGER, PEELED AND CHOPPED
2 TSP GROUND CORIANDER
1 TSP TURMERIC
400 G TIN CHOPPED TOMATOES
400 G TIN CHICKPEAS, RINSED AND DRAINED
400 ML TIN COCONUT MILK
200 ML WATER
HANDFUL FRESH CORIANDER, ROUGHLY CHOPPED
LEMON JUICE, TO TASTE

1 Peel the butternut squash, remove the seeds and chop into 1-inch pieces.

1 Remove and discard any thick stalks from the spinach leaves. Wash and roughly chop the leaves. Heat 2 tbsp of sunflower oil over a medium heat. Add the cumin seeds and mustard and allow to pop for 2 minutes. Add the onion and fry until soft, about 5 minutes. Add the garlic, chilli, ginger, ground coriander and turmeric and stir for a further minute. Add the butternut squash, tomatoes, 200 ml water and a pinch of salt. Bring to a boil, lower the heat, cover and cook for 15 minutes. Add the coconut milk, chickpeas and spinach leaves and cook for a further 5 minutes or until the squash and spinach are tender. Stir in the fresh coriander and season with salt and lemon juice to taste.

VEGETABLE GOULASH WITH HERB DUMPLINGS

This tasty, deeply savoury goulash is comforting on a cold day. The dumplings are lighter than you might think, and will have soaked up the delicious paprika-coloured juices.

SERVES 6 TO 8

FOR THE DUMPLINGS:
4 TBSP FINE WHOLEMEAL SPELT OR PASTRY FLOUR
4 TBSP WHITE SPELT OR PLAIN FLOUR
SEA SALT
2 TSP BAKING POWDER
55 G SUNFLOWER MARGARINE OR BUTTER
1 TBSP FRESH CHIVES, FINELY CHOPPED
1/2 TBSP FRESH OREGANO, FINELY CHOPPED
1/2 TBSP FRESH PARSLEY, FINELY CHOPPED

FOR THE GOULASH:
EXTRA VIRGIN OLIVE OIL
1 MEDIUM LEEK
1 LARGE CLOVE GARLIC (OPTIONAL)
4 MEDIUM CARROTS, CUT INTO CHUNKS
2 MEDIUM PARSNIPS, CUT INTO CHUNKS
1 SMALL TURNIP, CUT INTO CHUNKS
55 G BARLEY
4 TSP TOMATO PUREE
400 G CHOPPED TOMATOES
2 TSP PAPRIKA
2 BAY LEAVES
SEA SALT
2 VEGETABLE STOCK CUBES
3 MEDIUM POTATOES, CUT INTO CHUNKS
400 G TIN OF RED KIDNEY BEANS
400 G TIN OF CANNELLINI BEANS
FRESH PARSLEY FOR GARNISH

1 Make the dumplings. Place both of the flours, a pinch of sea salt and the baking powder into a large bowl. Mix. With your fingertips, rub in the margarine until the mix resembles breadcrumbs. Stir in the chives, oregano and parsley. Gradually add 4 tsp cold water and with your fingertips bring the mix together to form a soft dough. Do not knead. Set aside.

2 Wash the leek well and dice both the white and green parts. Heat 2 tbsp olive oil in a large pot and the leeks over a medium heat cook for 3 minutes. Add the garlic and cook for 30 seconds. Add the carrots, parsnip and turnip. Wash the barley and add to the pot along with the tomato puree, tomatoes, paprika, bay leaves and a pinch of salt. Stir the 2 vegetable stock cubes into 1 litre of boiled water. Pour into the pot, bring to a boil. Lower the heat, add the potatoes, cover tightly and simmer for 5 minutes.

3 Take pieces of the dumpling dough and roll into 2½ cm balls. Stir the kidney beans and cannellini beans into the simmering goulash. Arrange the dumplings on top of the goulash, put the lid back on and continue to simmer for a further 10 minutes. Turn the dumplings over and simmer for a further 5 minutes. The dumplings will double in size.

4 Check the seasoning. Serve with a sprinkling of parsley and paprika.

SPICED SWEET POTATO AND CHICKPEA STEW

Rich in flavour but mild in heat, this stew is a real family favourite.

SERVES 6
450 G COOKED CHICKPEAS
1 LARGE SWEET POTATO, ABOUT 400G
1/2 BUTTERNUT SQUASH OR PUMPKIN, ABOUT 400 G
2 MEDIUM RED ONIONS, DICED
4 CLOVES GARLIC, FINELY CHOPPED
1 RED CHILLI, DESEEDED AND FINELY CHOPPED
2 TSP CORIANDER SEEDS
2 TSP CUMIN SEEDS
1 TSP BLACK MUSTARD SEEDS
1 1/2 TSP TURMERIC
2 1/2 CM PIECE FRESH GINGER, PEELED AND FINELY CHOPPED
400 G TIN CHOPPED TOMATOES
2 TBSP FRESH CORIANDER, ROUGHLY CHOPPED
UNREFINED SUNFLOWER OIL
SEA SALT

1 Place the cumin seeds and coriander seeds in a dry frying pan and toast for about 5 minutes over a medium heat. Remove and grind finely in a mortar and pestle, or clean coffee grinder.

2 Heat the oil in a large pot over a medium heat and sauté the onion until soft but not brown. Add the mustard seeds and allow to pop for a few seconds and then add the garlic, chilli, ground cumin and coriander, turmeric, and ginger and cook for a further 2 minutes. Peel the sweet potato and pumpkin or butternut squash and chop into bite-size pieces. Add to the pot along with the chopped tomatoes and cooked chickpeas. Add 500 ml water and a pinch of sea salt. Bring to a boil, then lower heat to a gentle simmer. Cover and cook until the squash is tender, about 15 minutes. Season well and stir in the fresh coriander just before serving.

3 Serve with brown basmati rice. Also good with quinoa, fragrant rice or bulgur wheat.

Grains

In the West these days, we often rely on the same refined starches to accompany our meals day after day. Wholegrains are easy to find, economical and good for you, and it's worth trying out a couple to see which you and your family enjoy the most. My advice is to get the very best quality, organic grain you can find, and if needs be, to prioritise this over buying organic veg. You'll really notice the difference.

Grains offer a wealth of vitamins and minerals that white rice and pasta simply don't bring to your table. Some of these dishes are well-rounded accompaniments to your main meal, and others are plain, intended to be used in and served along with the recipes in this book, to be topped with stews, sauces and hearty vegetables.

Grains can take a bit more time to cook, but no longer than it would take you to make the meal you're serving with them, so get your grains on and then cook up your main dish – the finished grains can sit covered in a hot pot if they're finished before you are.

BARLEY

Barley has a lovely chewy texture and is easily digested.

SERVES 6
250 G BARLEY
UNREFINED SUNFLOWER OR RAPESEED OIL
1 SMALL ONION, FINELY DICED
SEA SALT
FRESH PARSLEY, FINELY CHOPPED, TO GARNISH

1 Wash the barley. Heat 2 tsp unrefined sunflower oil in a heavy-bottomed pot and sauté the onion until soft but not browned. Add the barley, 300 ml water and a pinch of sea salt. Bring to a boil, cover tightly, lower the heat and simmer for 30 minutes. Allow to rest for 5 minutes. Stir well before serving and garnish with finely chopped fresh parsley.

BULGUR

Bulgur is light and fluffy, with a complex, nutty taste.

SERVES 6
250 G BULGUR
UNREFINED SUNFLOWER OIL
1 SMALL ONION, FINELY DICED
SEA SALT
FRESH PARSLEY, FINELY CHOPPED, TO GARNISH

1 Wash the bulgur. Heat 1 tsp sunflower oil in a heavy-bottomed pot and sauté the onion until soft but not browned. Add the bulgur, 250 ml water and a pinch of sea salt. Bring to a boil, cover tightly, lower the heat and simmer for 20 minutes. Allow to sit for 5 minutes. Stir well before serving and garnish with finely chopped fresh parsley.

TIP: Leftover bulgur is lovely pan-fried and seasoned with a little soy sauce.

BUCKWHEAT WITH CARROT AND SPINACH

Buckwheat suits all kinds of hearty cooking in the colder months.

SERVES 6
250 G BUCKWHEAT
½ ONION, DICED
UNREFINED SUNFLOWER OIL
SOYA SAUCE
1 CARROT
BABY SPINACH LEAVES, WASHED

1 Place the buckwheat in a bowl and wash well. Drain. Place 500 ml water in a heavy-bottomed pot with a tight-fitting lid. Bring to a boil. Add 2 tbsp soya sauce to the boiling water along with the onion and the washed buckwheat. Bring back to a boil, cover, lower the heat and simmer for 30 minutes. Roughly grate the carrot, either in a food processor or by hand. Stir up the cooked buckwheat and add the grated carrot and a big handful of spinach leaves. Mix well and season with soya sauce.

TIP: Leftover buckwheat is delicious fried in a pan.

FRAGRANT RICE

Fragrant rice is the perfect accompaniment for curries and stews. It also works well in rice salads. The light spices add a subtle, well-rounded flavour. If you are placing it in a serving bowl on the table, leave the cinnamon stick and bayleaf in – it makes for a nice rustic touch.

SERVES 6
450 G BROWN BASMATI RICE, OR ANY LONG-GRAIN RICE
2 TSP SUNFLOWER OIL
2 TSP SUNFLOWER MARGARINE
1 ONION, HALVED AND SLICED
4 CARDAMOM PODS
2 CLOVES
1 CINNAMON STICK
¹/₂ TSP TURMERIC
1 BAY LEAF
SEA SALT

1 Wash the rice well and drain. In a heavy-bottomed pot, heat the oil and the margarine. Sauté the onion until soft. Add rice, cardamom pods, cloves, cinnamon stick, turmeric and bay leaf. Sauté for 1 minute. Add a pinch of salt and pour in 700 ml water. Bring to a boil, cover, lower the heat and simmer for 45 minutes. Allow to stand for 5 minutes. Fluff up the rice. Remove spices. Serve.

MILLET WITH SWEET POTATO AND CAULIFLOWER

Millet is a light grain, gluten-free and alkaline. It's a good food for anyone suffering from allergies.

SERVES 6
250 G MILLET
SEA SALT
1 SMALL ONION, FINELY DICED
100 G CAULIFLOWER, CUT INTO FLORETS
100 G SWEET POTATO, DICED
FRESH PARSLEY, TO GARNISH

1 Wash the millet. Place in a heavy-bottomed pot with the onion, cauliflower, sweet potato and a pinch of salt. Add 200 ml water. Bring to a boil, cover tightly, lower the heat and simmer for 30 minutes. Allow to stand for 5 minutes, remove the lid and stir well. Check the seasoning. Serve garnished with chopped fresh parsley.

QUINOA

Quinoa is a quick, light grain to cook. It is a high-protein food, perfect for vegetarians or vegans.

SERVES 6
UNREFINED SUNFLOWER OIL
½ ONION, DICED (OPTIONAL)
250 G QUINOA
SEA SALT
FRESH PARSLEY

1 In a heavy-bottomed pot, heat 2 tsp sunflower oil. If using, sauté the onion until soft but not brown, about 5 minutes. (Onion makes a nice addition if you're serving this plain as a side dish. If you're using as part of another recipe, omit.) Wash the quinoa well and drain off the water. Add to the pot with the onion, along with a pinch of sea salt and 250 ml water. Bring to a boil, lower the heat and cover tightly. Simmer for 15 minutes. Leave to stand for a further 15 minutes. Do not be tempted to remove the lid for the 30 minutes, as the quinoa is steaming. When the cooking time is up, remove the lid and fluff up the quinoa.

2 If serving plain as a side dish, garnish with fresh parsley to serve.

Side Dishes

We're pretty open-minded when it comes to how, when and where our food should be eaten. When you run a deli, you get used to the idea that some customers will place the same order time and again, while others will cobble a meal together out of what takes their fancy that day. As all of our food is good for you, there's really no reason not to pick and choose any combination of the dishes in this book that you like.

It always seems a little sad to relinquish some of your favourites to 'side orders', but sometimes the practicalities of running a busy lunch counter win out. So consider the following recipes as ways to sneak a few more veggies or another bit of protein in to balance your meal, or as the stars of the show in their own right. Simple and to the point, these are the things your family will come to ask for, and your guests will wonder quite how you got them to taste so good.

OCCOLI WITH TOASTED HAZELNUTS AND SOYA SAUCE

e dishes that everyone picks at until it's all gone, even when hunger has long since passed.

SERVES 6
25 G HAZELNUTS
1 HEAD OF BROCCOLI
UNREFINED SUNFLOWER OIL
3 SPRING ONIONS, SLICED
SOYA SAUCE

1 Preheat oven to Gas 5/190°C/375°F. Place the hazelnuts onto a baking tray. Put in a preheated oven to toast for 15 minutes. Chop roughly.

2 Wash broccoli and cut into florets, leaving some of the stalk attached. Place into a pot with 1 cm of water. Bring to a boil, lower the heat, cover tightly and simmer for 5–8 minutes. The broccoli should be tender but not mushy. Set aside.

3 Heat 1 tbsp sunflower oil in a pot and sauté the spring onions for 1 minute. Add the steamed broccoli florets, the toasted hazelnuts and 1 tbsp soya sauce. Toss well until the broccoli is heated through.

4 Check the seasoning adding more soya sauce if you wish. Serve.

TIP: This side dish makes a good lunch box salad, as it's great cold. Accompany with one of the grain salads for a balanced meal.

TIP: Replace the broccoli with French beans – also delicious.

TIP: Toast all the hazelnuts in the packet at the one time and keep what you don't need in a jar in your cupboard. Nuts are also easier to digest when roasted.

HALLOUMI CHEESE WITH FRESH BASIL

Halloumi is a curd-like, salty cheese made with cow's, goat's and sheep's milk and vegetable rennet. It is prepared by frying on a pan or barbecued to bring out its lovely, chewy texture. It is perfect in sandwiches or on a skewer with vegetables as it doesn't fall apart. It has a very good shelf life, so I always keep some in the fridge for that unexpected visitor. Just brush with olive oil and fry on a pan or follow the recipe below.

250 G HALLOUMI CHEESE
2 TBSP FRESH BASIL, FINELY CHOPPED
2 TBSP EXTRA VIRGIN OLIVE OIL
LEMON JUICE

1 Mix the fresh basil with the olive oil in a dish. Slice the halloumi cheese into ¼ cm slices and leave to marinate in the olive oil and basil for a few minutes.

2 Heat a pan over a medium heat. Lay the halloumi slices in the pan, but do not overcrowd the pan. Fry each side until golden brown. Repeat until all the slices are fried.

3 Spoon some of the basil and oil marinade and a squeeze of lemon juice over the fried cheese and serve.

ASIAN GREENS

Cabbage and kale were the only greens grown in Ireland at one time, but now all the lovely light greens in the Asian stores are grown here too. All cabbages do well with strong flavours and brief cooking to create a fresh, vibrant dish. Serve with a plain grain (p. 124) as a bed for your tofu (p. 140) and greens for a fast, one-bowl meal, and try out your chopstick skills!

CABBAGE WITH GARLIC, CHILLI AND SHALLOTS

This does winter kales and pak choi proud, too (see photo on page 138).

SERVES 6
COLD-PRESSED SESAME OIL
2 SHALLOTS
2 CLOVES GARLIC, SLIVERED
1 TSP RED CHILLI, DESEEDED AND SLICED THINLY
1 HEAD YORK OR SPRING CABBAGE
SEA SALT

1 Prepare the cabbage. Remove the outer leaves and the thick, hard stalk. Cut the heart in half. Wash well. Slice the leaves thinly and shred the heart.

2 In a large heavy-bottomed pot, heat 2 tbsp sesame oil. Fry the shallots, garlic and chilli for 1 minute and add the cabbage a few handfuls at a time, stirring constantly until the cabbage is coated in the chilli, garlic and shallots. Season with a pinch of sea salt and add 4 tbsp water to the pot. Cover and over a medium heat, cook the cabbage for 5–7 minutes or until the cabbage has wilted completely. Uncover and turn up the heat, stirring the cabbage for another 1–2 minutes.

3 This cabbage is delicious as it is or tossed with cooked buckwheat noodles (soba).

TIP: Instead of salt, season this dish with a sprinkling of soya sauce at the end of cooking.

PAK CHOI WITH COURGETTE, ONION AND GINGER

Served on noodles, this side is quick to prepare. It's a great source of vitamins and is packed with flavour (see photo, p. 138).

SERVES 6
UNREFINED SESAME OIL
2 ONIONS
2 CLOVES GARLIC
1 COURGETTE
3 HEADS PAK CHOI
FRESH GINGER
SOYA SAUCE
TOASTED SESAME SEEDS

1 Peel the onions, slice in half and cut in half moon slices. Thinly slice the garlic cloves. Wash and slice the courgette in half lengthwise. Slice on the diagonal.

2 Cut the end off of the pak choi and slice thinly. Separate the larger leaves and slice in half lengthwise. Heat 2 tbsp oil in a pan and add the onions. Sauté for 1 minute. Add the garlic and courgette and sauté for 2 more minutes. Add the pak choi and sauté for 3 minutes or until the leaves of the pak choi have wilted. Add 1 tsp finely grated ginger and 1 tbsp soya sauce and sauté for a further minute. Check the seasoning and serve sprinkled with toasted sesame seeds.

3 For a quick meal, serve these vegetables with some pan-fried tofu (p. 140) and a grain or noodles.

ARLIC, CHILLI AND SHALLOTS, PAGE 136

PAK CHOI WITH COURGETTE, ONION AND GINGER, PAGE 137

PAN-FRIED TOFU WITH SPRING ONION AND GINGER, PAGE 141

TOFU

Tofu is a curd made from soya beans. Soya beans are full of valuable vitamins and amino acids and are above all a good-quality protein. To make soybeans more digestible they are made into tofu. The beans are soaked, blended, cooked and then mixed with a solidifier called 'nigari'. Nigari acts like the culture used for making yoghurt or rennet in cheesemaking, allowing the curd to be separated from the whey and made into small blocks.

The best thing about tofu is its versatility; it can be baked, steamed, deep-fried and sautéed, and these simple recipes take the mystery out of how to cook it while staying true to its Asian roots.

BAKED TOFU WITH SOYA SAUCE

If you don't like to deep fry, dice the tofu into cubes, pat with paper towel and place in an oven proof dish. Toss with some unrefined sunflower oil and soy sauce and bake in a hot oven, Gas 7/220°C/425°F for 20–30 minutes until it develops a chewy texture. Season with more soya sauce if it needs it.

PAN-FRIED SESAME TOFU

This is a quick, tasty way to add protein to your meal.

SERVES 6
3 CUBES OF TOFU
3 TBSP SOYA SAUCE
¹/₃ TSP FRESH GINGER, FINELY GRATED
4 TSP SESAME SEEDS
3 TBSP BROWN RICE FLOUR
UNREFINED SUNFLOWER OIL, OR UNREFINED RAPE SEED OIL

1 Slice each cube of tofu in half, and slice each half into 4 slices. You will have 24 slices of tofu. Mix the ginger with the soya sauce. Place the tofu slices in a dish and add the soya sauce and ginger and marinate for 20 minutes. After 10 minutes turn over the slices to marinate each side.

2 Mix the sesame seeds and the rice flour together. Heat some oil in a pan. Press the tofu slices in the rice flour and sesame seed mix and coat both sides. Lay the coated tofu slices onto the hot pan. Do not overcrowd the pan. Fry each side of the tofu slice until they are browned. Set aside the fried tofu on a plate until all the slices are coated and fried. Place 12 of the fried tofu into the pan with half of the marinade and toss the tofu in the soya sauce over a high heat until the marinade has reduced. Remove from the pan and keep warm in a preheated oven while you toss the rest of the tofu in the marinade.

PAN-FRIED TOFU WITH SPRING ONION AND GINGER

See photo on page 139.

SERVES 6
3 CUBES TOFU
UNREFINED SUNFLOWER OR RAPESEED OIL
3 SPRING ONIONS, WHITE AND GREEN PARTS, SLICED
⅓ TSP FINELY GRATED GINGER
3 TBSP SOYA SAUCE

1 Slice the cubes of tofu in half. Slice each half into 4 slices. You should have 24 slices. To squeeze the excess water out of the tofu, cover 2 large plates in plenty of kitchen paper. Lay the tofu on the paper and cover with more kitchen paper. Place a large plate on top of each, and weigh the plates down with tinned veg or a heavy pot. Set aside for 30 minutes.

2 Mix the ginger with the soya sauce.

3 Heat 1 tbsp sunflower oil in a large pan. Lay 12 tofu slices in the pan and fry each side until lightly golden, approx. 5 minutes. Add half of the sliced spring onions to the pan with the tofu. Pour in half of the soya and ginger sauce and toss, allowing the liquid to reduce a little. Place the tofu on a serving plate and keep warm in the oven or under the grill. Wipe the pan and repeat with the rest of the tofu slices.

TIP: If you like some heat, add half a sliced chilli to the pan with the spring onions.

DEEP-FRIED TOFU WITH SOYA SAUCE

Deep-fried tofu has a great chewy texture for using in salads, soup or stir-fry. Deep-fry a batch and it will keep for 1 week in the fridge. Season with soya sauce before storing.

SERVES 2
1 CUBE TOFU
SUNFLOWER OIL FOR FRYING
SOYA SAUCE, TO TASTE

1 Slice 1 cube of tofu into 4 slices down the cube and 4 slices across until you have 16 small cubes. Set aside on plenty of kitchen paper. Pour 3 inches of sunflower oil in a pot or use a deep fat fryer and heat until very hot but not smoking. Pat the tofu with more kitchen paper. Lower tofu into the hot oil and fry until golden brown, approx. 10 minutes. Remove and drain on some kitchen paper. Place in a bowl and toss in soya sauce to taste.

FRENCH BEANS WITH PARMESAN

This is a very simple side dish that tastes great and is amazingly popular with children. Cook extra, you will be asked for more.

SERVES 6
600 G FRENCH BEANS
SEA SALT
1 TSP BUTTER
VEGETARIAN PARMESAN-STYLE CHEESE, FINELY GRATED

1 Remove the stalks from the French beans. Place in a pot with 1 cm water and a pinch of sea salt. Cover tightly, bring to a boil, lower the heat and simmer for 3–4 minutes, until the beans are tender but not soft. Drain, add 1 tsp butter and half of the cheese. Toss. Place on plates and serve sprinkled with the remaining cheese.

TIP: Many hard cheeses have a flavour similar to Parmesan; one of our favourites is Desmond cheese from Co. Cork, which is made with vegetarian rennet.

ROASTING VEGETABLES

Roasted vegetables are as tasty as they are because the high heat of the oven intensifies their flavours and draws out their natural sugars. Beyond the Sunday lunch, roast veg can be used as the star of a simple cold salad, in turnovers, tarts, and as the basis for magnificent puréed soups.

You can of course mix and match the veg and their seasonings, but check that the veg you're roasting together has the same cooking time, or you'll have some veg underdone and others too crispy.

The key with roasting it to get your oven hot – preheat your oven to **Gas 7/220°C/425°F** for all of these variations.

BUTTERNUT SQUASH WITH CHILLI

SERVES 6
750 G BUTTERNUT SQUASH
1 CHILLI, DESEEDED AND SLICED
1 SPRIG ROSEMARY
EXTRA VIRGIN OLIVE OIL
SEA SALT

1 Peel the butternut squash halve and remove the seeds. Cut into 2½ cm slices. Place in an ovenproof dish. Add the chilli and chop the rosemary and add to the squash along with 2 tbsp olive oil, and a pinch of sea salt. Toss well to coat the squash. Place on the top shelf of a hot oven and bake for 25 minutes until the squash is cooked through. Toss one last time before serving.

PARSNIPS WITH AGAVE

Sticky and chewy at the thin end and light and fluffy at the fat end, these sweet parsnips are always a crowd-pleaser.

SERVES 6
4 MEDIUM PARSNIPS
2 TSP FRESH THYME LEAVES
EXTRA VIRGIN OLIVE OIL
SEA SALT
2 TSP AGAVE SYRUP, MAPLE SYRUP OR HONEY

1 Peel the parsnips, slice in half lengthwise and cut into chunks. Place in an ovenproof dish. Sprinkle over the fresh thyme, 2 tbsp olive oil and a good pinch of sea salt. Toss well. Place on the top shelf of a hot oven and roast for 30 minutes or until the parsnips are tender. Toss in 2 tsp agave syrup and serve.

VEGETABLES WITH OLIVE OIL AND FRESH THYME

SERVES 6
2 RED ONIONS
1 CLOVE GARLIC, MINCED
1 CARROT
DAIKON, SAME AMOUNT AS CARROT
FRESH THYME
SEA SALT
EXTRA VIRGIN OLIVE OIL
100 G BUTTERNUT SQUASH
½ HEAD MEDIUM BROCCOLI, ABOUT 12 BITE-SIZE FLORETS

1 Peel and quarter the red onions. Place in an ovenproof dish along with the garlic. Slice the carrots in half lengthwise, then slice on the diagonal into 1 cm thick pieces, and add to the dish. Do the same with the daikon. Add 2 tsp fresh thyme leaves and a good pinch of sea salt. Pour over 2 tbsp olive oil and toss well. Place on the top shelf of the preheated oven and roast. Cut the squash into chunks. After 15 minutes, remove the vegetables from the oven and add the squash and the broccoli. Toss well. Return to the oven and roast for a further 20–30 minutes until the vegetables are tender. See photo, p. 147.

AUBERGINE WITH RED ONION AND PAPRIKA

For a simple dish, this is really stunning on the plate – shiny blacks and purples with gorgeous brick-red juices from the paprika. In fact, it's the base of our roast aubergine soup (p. 61), and started as a side dish only when our chef Zenon commented on how lovely it looked just out of the oven.

SERVES 6
2 AUBERGINES
3 RED ONIONS, QUARTERED
1 SPRIG ROSEMARY
2 CLOVES OF GARLIC, SLICED
PAPRIKA
EXTRA VIRGIN OLIVE OIL
SEA SALT

1 Rinse the aubergine and remove the stalk. Chop into 5 cm pieces. Place into an ovenproof dish. Pull the leaves from the rosemary sprig and add to the aubergine along with the red onion, garlic, a good pinch of paprika, 2 tbsp extra virgin olive oil, and a pinch of sea salt. Toss well. Place on the top shelf of the preheated oven for 30 minutes until the aubergine is tender. Check the seasoning and toss well before serving.

SWEET POTATO WITH ROSEMARY

Sweet potatoes are an excellent source of vitamin A and a good source of potassium and vitamin C, vitamin B6, folic acid and copper. The deep orange colour will liven up any meal.

SERVES 6
750 G SWEET POTATO
1 SPRIG FRESH ROSEMARY
EXTRA VIRGIN OLIVE OIL
SEA SALT

1 Peel the sweet potato and slice into 2 cm rounds. Place in an ovenproof dish. Chop the rosemary and add to the sweet potato along with 2 tbsp olive oil, and a pinch of sea salt. Toss well to coat the sweet potato. Place on the top shelf of the oven and bake for 30 minutes until the sweet potato is cooked through. Toss one last time before serving.

2 For a more complex flavour, omit the salt and sprinkle the baked sweet potato with soya sauce.

RATATOUILLE VEGETABLES

This recipe is more substantial than the others here, and makes a great lunch of light dinner with some good crusty bread to mop up the juices. Serve with pan-fried halloumi cheese with basil (p. 135), crumbled feta cheese, or add some cooked chickpeas.

SERVES 6

2 RED ONION, CUT INTO 2 CM DICE
1 SMALL AUBERGINE, CUT INTO 2 CM DICE
1 COURGETTE, CUT INTO 2 CM DICE
1 RED PEPPER, CUT INTO 2 CM DICE
2 CLOVES GARLIC, CHOPPED
EXTRA VIRGIN OLIVE OIL
SEA SALT
1 TSP DRIED BASIL, OR DRIED OREGANO OR DRIED ITALIAN HERBS
1 400G TIN OF TOMATOES, CHOPPED
FRESH BASIL

1 Place the red onion, aubergine, courgette, red pepper and garlic in an ovenproof dish. Add 3 tbsp olive oil, and a good pinch each of dried basil and sea salt. Toss well to coat all the vegetables. Place on the top shelf of the preheated oven for 20 minutes. Remove from the oven and stir in the tomatoes. Return to the oven for a further 15 minutes until the vegetables are soft.

2 Remove from the oven and toss in 1 tbsp chopped fresh basil. Check the seasoning and serve.

Desserts

My siblings and I grew up in a macrobiotic household, but that isn't nearly as strict as it sounds; 'all things in moderation' is one of its mantras. Desserts have as big a role in a healthy, wholefood diet as they do in any other. Eating treats you've made yourself when you crave something sweet also prevents you from wolfing down a soon-forgotten chocolate bar or absentmindedly munching your way through biscuits in the office. These recipes give you something to savour, and baking, particularly with and for family, is a joy.

Lots of these recipes travel well, so they'll become a must for picnics, school lunchboxes and treating your colleagues. Others are attractive for special occasions like Christmas and birthdays, and may well become part of your family's traditions as they are for mine.

The best part is that even though you're indulging yourself with cakes and biscuits, you're also benefitting from the goodness of wholegrain flours, natural sweeteners, seeds, nuts and dried fruit. Oh, and just a little chocolate...

BAKED PEARS WITH WARM BLUEBERRY SYRUP

Warm, sweet pears are covered in a deep purple blueberry syrup for this stunning dessert, packed with nutritious ingredients from the almonds and dried apricots with their touch of toffee flavours.

SERVES 6

3 LARGE PEARS, FIRM BUT NOT HARD (CONFERENCE OR WILLIAM ARE EXCELLENT)
55 G GROUND ALMONDS
40 G UNSULPHURED DRIED APRICOTS
40 G SUNDRIED RAISINS
25 G FLAKED ALMONDS
1¹/₂ TBSP AGAVE SYRUP, MAPLE SYRUP OR HONEY
¹/₂ TSP NATURAL ALMOND ESSENCE
300 ML APPLE JUICE

FOR THE SYRUP:
125 G PUNNET BLUEBERRIES
2 TBSP AGAVE SYRUP
1 TSP KUZU OR ARROWROOT POWDER

1 Peel the pears and slice in half, slicing down from the stalk. Using a teaspoon, scoop out the pips from the centre, leaving a 2 cm hollow. Gently scrape out the stalk. Preheat the oven to Gas 5/190°C/375°F.

2 Place the prepared pears in an ovenproof dish.

3 Wash the apricots and chop into very small pieces. Place in a bowl along with the raisins, flaked almonds, almond essence, ground almonds and 1½ tbsp agave syrup. Mix well with your fingers and bring together into a stiff dough. Press the stuffing into the hollowed-out centre of each pear half, dividing the stuffing equally among all the pears. Pour the apple juice around the pears. Cover with tin foil. Place into the preheated oven and bake for 25–30 minutes until the pears are tender but not mushy. Remove the pears carefully to a plate and cover with tin foil to keep warm. Set the juice remaining in the dish aside to cool.

4 Blend the kuzu or arrowroot powder with the cooled apple juice. Add to the pot with the blueberries and 2 tbsp agave syrup. Bring to a boil and lower the heat and simmer until the blueberries burst, about 2 minutes. The syrup will thicken a little. Place the pears in individual serving bowls and spoon the blueberry syrup over each one.

5 This dessert is best served with natural yoghurt.

TIP: For anyone who doesn't need such sweet sweeteners, brown rice syrup is also delicious instead of the agave syrup.

SOFT-BAKE COOKIES

These cookies are so good – not sugary sweet, but satisfying. Definitely a 'more than one' cookie.

MAKES 10-20
250 G WHOLEMEAL SPELT FLOUR
1 TSP BAKING POWDER
SEA SALT
70 G SUNDRIED RAISINS, WASHED
125 G UNSULPHURED APRICOTS, WASHED AND CHOPPED
70 G CASHEW NUTS
70 G FLAKED ALMONDS
3 FREE RANGE EGGS
175 G SUNFLOWER MARGARINE
70 G APPLE CONCENTRATE
85 G MAPLE SYRUP
1 TSP VANILLA EXTRACT

1 Preheat oven to Gas 4/180°C/350°F.

2 Place the flour, baking powder, a pinch of salt, raisins, apricots, cashew nuts, flaked almonds in a large bowl. In a separate bowl beat the margarine with the maple syrup and apple concentrate with a wooden spoon for about 3 minutes. Whisk the eggs and add them gradually to the margarine mix, whisking all the time. Add the vanilla extract. Stir in the dry ingredients and mix well. Lightly oil a baking tray. Take dessertspoons of the cookie mixture and place on the prepared tray, leaving a 4 cm space between each mound. Dampen the back of the spoon and press down on the mounds to create a cookie shape. Bake for 25–30 minutes until golden brown. Place on a cooling tray to cool.

TIP: These cookies are great for children, but best to make them smaller for little hands, so spoon out the dough using a teaspoon instead.

CARROT AND WALNUT MUFFINS

Great for breakfast on the go, these muffins are nourishing and not too sweet, thanks to the apple concentrate.

MAKES 12
3 FREE RANGE EGGS
175 G SUNFLOWER MARGARINE
150 ML APPLE CONCENTRATE
1 ORANGE
85 G TOASTED WALNUTS, CHOPPED
55 G DATES, CHOPPED
175 G CARROT, FINELY GRATED
250 G WHOLEMEAL SPELT FLOUR
2 TSP BAKING POWDER
³/₄ TSP CINNAMON

1 Preheat oven to Gas 4/180°C/350°F. Oil and line a 12-cup muffin tray with paper cases. Lightly oil the paper cases. Whisk the eggs in a large bowl. Add the margarine and whisk until light and fluffy. Pour in the apple concentrate. Finely grate the rind of the orange and add to the bowl along with the chopped walnuts, chopped dates, grated carrot, and stir together. Sieve in the flour and baking powder and cinnamon into the wet mixture and stir well.

2 Spoon the muffin mix evenly into the prepared muffin cups.

3 Bake in the centre of the preheated oven for 40–45 minutes. The muffins should be springy to the touch.

4 These muffins don't need a topping, but you can use cream cheese icing (p. 175) or top with thick Greek yoghurt and a little orange zest.

TIP: This recipe will make a whole cake baked in a round 20 cm round baking tin.

ALMOND CAKES

Almond cakes are always popular; moist, succulent and wheat-free, they rise evenly and last well in a tin. Here we've given two variations on the theme, with a simple finger slice cake recipe for bake sales and large groups, and a more decadent full cake, Blazing Salads' own take on the classic bakewell tart. You can use other sweeteners, but I can't recommend maple syrup here strongly enough for its gorgeous, almost smoky taste.

ALMOND AND RASPBERRY FINGERS

This moist and sweet cake is perfect for lunch boxes and picnics. Popular with children and adults alike.

MAKES 20
FOR THE PASTRY:
175 G WHOLEMEAL SPELT FLOUR
SEA SALT
85 G SUNFLOWER MARGARINE

FOR THE FILLING:
4 FREE RANGE EGGS
1 TSP NATURAL ALMOND ESSENCE
100 ML MAPLE SYRUP (PLUS EXTRA FOR BRUSHING THE BAKED CAKE)
50 ML AGAVE SYRUP
150 G WHOLEMEAL SPELT FLOUR
150 G GROUND ALMONDS
1 TSP BAKING POWDER
100 ML RICE, SOYA OR COW'S MILK
25 G FLAKED ALMONDS
180 G SUGAR-FREE RASPBERRY JAM

1 Make the pastry. Place the flour in a large bowl. Stir in a pinch of salt. Rub in the margarine until the mix resembles breadcrumbs. Add 20 ml cold water and with your fingertips, bring the flour together until a ball of dough has formed. Wrap in cling film and place in the fridge to rest for 30 minutes.

2 Preheat oven to Gas 4/180°C/350°F.

3 Oil a 30 x 23 cm baking tray. On a well-floured surface, roll out the pastry into a rectangle and line the baking tray. Press the pastry into the base and sides of the tin and trim the edges. Prick the base with a fork and place in the preheated oven for 20 minutes until the pastry has become crisp but not browned.

4 While the pastry is in the oven, make the filling. In a large bowl whisk the eggs until light and fluffy. Add the almond essence and the margarine and whisk for 1 minute. Add the maple syrup and the agave syrup and whisk for a further 2 minutes. Add the spelt flour, ground almond and baking powder. Whisk together. Pour in the milk and whisk until smooth.

5 Spread the raspberry jam over the baked pastry base. Pour the almond mixture over the jam and spread out evenly into all the corners. Sprinkle with the flaked almonds and bake in the centre of the oven for 25–30 minutes until golden brown. Remove and place on a cooling tray. When cool, brush with maple syrup and slice into 20 finger-length pieces.

BLAZING SALADS BAKEWELL TART, PAGE 162

BLAZING SALADS BAKEWELL TART

This recipe is adapted from the traditional bakewell tart recipe. I tried it with maple syrup and I find it gives a great flavour and moistness to the cake. It is worth a little bit of extra effort for those special occasions (see previous page).

SERVES 8 TO 10

FOR THE PASTRY:
175 G WHOLEMEAL SPELT FLOUR
SEA SALT
85 G UNSALTED BUTTER, CHILLED

FOR THE FILLING:
180 G SUGAR-FREE RASPBERRY JAM
175 G UNSALTED BUTTER
4 FREE RANGE EGGS PLUS 2 EGG YOLKS
175 ML MAPLE SYRUP (PLUS A LITTLE FOR BRUSHING THE BAKED TART)
175 G GROUND ALMONDS
1¹/₂ TSP NATURAL ALMOND ESSENCE
55 G FLAKED ALMONDS

1 Sieve the flour and a pinch of sea salt into a large bowl. Dice the butter into cubes and add to the bowl and rub with your finger tips until the mix resembles bread crumbs. Add 2 dessertspoons cold water. With your finger tips bring the mix together to form a ball of dough. Wrap in cling film and place in the fridge to chill for half an hour.

2 Oil a 28 cm flan cake tin or glass flan dish. On a lightly floured surface, roll out the pastry and line the oiled flan tin. Press the pastry into the sides of the tin until all air pockets are gone. Trim the top edge of the pastry. With your forefingers, press the pastry into the fluted sides of the tin. Place in the fridge to chill for 20 minutes.

3 Preheat oven to Gas 2/150°C/300°F.

4 Place the butter for the filling in an ovenproof dish and melt in the oven. Whisk the eggs in a large bowl. Add the maple syrup, ground almonds, and almond essence and whisk well. Whisk in the melted butter. Spoon the raspberry jam onto the chilled pastry base and spread out evenly. Pour the filling onto the prepared pastry case. Place in the centre of the oven. After 10 minutes, sprinkle the flaked almonds over the tart and continue to bake for a further 20 minutes until the tart is golden and just set in the middle. The almonds are sprinkled on the tart 10 minutes after baking as they sink into the filling if sprinkled on at the start of the baking.

CHOCOLATE SEED BARS
WITH CRANBERRIES AND ORANGE

We introduced these seed bars at Christmas in the deli, and the flavours really complement each other. Great for Christmastime travel, or wrapped up for a homemade gift.

MAKES 12
125 G PUMPKIN SEEDS
175 G SUNFLOWER SEEDS
70 G SESAME SEEDS
150 G 70% DARK CHOCOLATE
70 G DRIED CRANBERRIES
100 G SUNFLOWER MARGARINE
3 TBSP AGAVE SYRUP
1 TBSP ORANGE PEEL

1 Preheat oven to Gas 5/190°C/375°F.

2 Oil and line a 20 cm or 23 cm square baking tin with greaseproof paper, and lightly oil the paper. Place the seeds on a baking tray and roast in a preheated oven for 15 minutes until lightly golden.

3 Break the chocolate into squares and place in a glass or metal bowl with the sunflower margarine, dried cranberries, and agave syrup. Chop the orange peel finely, and add to the bowl. Rest the bowl over a pot of lightly boiling water and melt. Stir occasionally. Do not let the base of the bowl touch the water, as it will effect the smoothness of the melted chocolate.

4 Place 175 g of the toasted seeds into a food processor and blend, or grind using a mortar and pestle.

5 When the chocolate has melted completely remove the bowl from the pot and add the ground seeds and the remaining roasted whole seeds. Stir well. Press the mixture into the square baking tin using a metal spoon dipped in water, pressing down lightly on the warm chocolate and seed mixture. Continue until the mixture is smooth and even. Place in the fridge and allow to set.

6 Cut into squares and enjoy. The bars will keep well in an airtight container in the fridge.

TIP: For a less Christmassy variation, try replacing the cranberries with raisins, using honey or maple syrup instead of agave and leaving out the orange peel – a real store cupboard special when you need a treat in a pinch.

PLUM COBBLER WITH FLAKED ALMONDS

Cobbler is an old-fashioned dessert that is particularly popular in the US, made with seasonal fruits baked with a scone-like topping dropped on top to make like cobblestones. I love using red plums because the ruby-coloured juice bubbles up during baking. This is best in the autumn, when plums are at their peak and plentiful.

SERVES 6

FOR THE FILLING:
750 G PLUMS
1 TBSP AGAVE SYRUP
3 TBSP APPLE CONCENTRATE

FOR THE TOPPING:
225 G WHITE SPELT FLOUR OR PLAIN WHITE FLOUR
PINCH OF SEA SALT
2 TSP OF BAKING POWDER
1 TSP GROUND CINNAMON, PLUS EXTRA TO SPRINKLE ON TOP
110 G SUNFLOWER MARGARINE
1 TBSP AGAVE SYRUP
175 ML BUTTERMILK
60 G FLAKED ALMONDS

1 Preheat oven to Gas 5/190°C/375°F.

2 Prepare the plums. Wash well, and using a sharp knife, slit the plums all the way around through to the pip. Using both hands twist and pull apart. Remove the stone. Cut into quarters. Place in a 23 cm baking dish. Stir in the agave syrup, coating all the pieces. Set aside.

3 Make the topping. Sift the flour and place into a large bowl along with a pinch of sea salt, baking powder and cinnamon. Rub in the margarine with your fingertips until the mix resembles breadcrumbs. Stir the agave syrup into the buttermilk and pour into the flour mixture until a sticky mix forms.

4 Pour the apple concentrate into 200 ml water and stir. Pour over the plums and agave syrup. Spoon the dough mixture over the plums keeping in uneven. Scatter the flaked almonds over and sprinkle with a pinch of cinnamon.

5 Bake for 30 minutes or until golden brown.

TIP: This dish is also delicious with pears or fresh apricots.

GUR CAKE

Gur cake is a fruit slice traditionally made in Dublin. It was made from left-over stale bread or cake and baked with dried fruit. It was one of the cheapest cakes to buy from the baker, and was popular with young lads 'on the gur' – mitching from school. NB: this recipe should be started the night before, in order to give the dried fruit time to soak.

MAKES 12-16 SLICES

FOR THE FILLING:
200 G SUNDRIED RAISINS
200 G CURRANTS
200 G SULTANAS
1 TEABAG
350 G BREADCRUMBS
4 TBSP AGAVE SYRUP OR APPLE CONCENTRATE
2 TSP MIXED SPICE

FOR THE PASTRY:
350 G WHOLEMEAL SPELT OR FINE WHOLEMEAL FLOUR
SEA SALT
150 G SUNFLOWER MARGARINE
20-30 ML COLD WATER

1 Wash the raisins, currants and sultanas and place in a large bowl along with a teabag and boiling water and soak overnight or for 6–8 hours.

2 Make the pastry. In a large bowl place the flour and a pinch of salt and rub in the margarine until the mix resembles breadcrumbs. Add the water gradually and mix using your fingertips until the pastry comes away from the sides of the bowl and forms a ball. Wrap the ball of dough in cling film and place in the fridge to rest for 30 minutes.

3 Preheat oven to Gas 4/180°C/350°F.

4 Squeeze the teabag into the soaked fruit and discard. Add the breadcrumbs, agave syrup and mixed spice to the fruit. Mix well. Oil a 23 cm square baking tin.

5 Take the pastry out of the fridge and roll half of it out on a lightly floured surface, using the baking tin as a template. Cut the pastry slightly larger than the size of the tin and line the base of the tin with it, pressing well into the sides and corners. Pour in the fruit mixture and press down evenly with the palm of your hand. Roll out the other half of the pastry, again to a size slightly larger than the tin.

6 Place the pastry on top of the fruit mix and press firmly around the edges. Place in the centre of the preheated oven and bake for 40 minutes or until the top is golden brown. Slice into 12-16 pieces to serve.

TIP: This cake keeps very well and is great for picnics or long journeys. It also freezes well.

CHOCOLATE TRAYBAKE

This is a great cake to make with children – you have their attention because there's chocolate involved. After that, it's a great way for them to learn how to crack an egg, separate the egg, whisk the egg… There's flour sifting, which is always fun, you can show them how to mix the ingredients with a light hand to make the cake lighter. Depending on their ages, there's something for everyone to do, even oiling the tin and breaking up the chocolate. Best of all, they get to lick a tasty bowl and spoon at the end.

MAKES 18-20 PIECES

250 G SUNFLOWER MARGARINE
250 G AGAVE SYRUP
4 FREE RANGE EGGS
250 G WHITE SPELT FLOUR
2 TSP BAKING POWDER
PINCH OF SALT
4 TBSP COCOA POWDER
60 ML MILK

FOR THE TOPPING:

4 TBSP FRESH CREAM
150 G 70% DARK CHOCOLATE

1 Oil a 30 x 22 cm Swiss roll baking tin. Line with greaseproof paper, and lightly oil the paper. Preheat oven to Gas 3/170°C/325 °F.

2 In a large mixing bowl, cream together the margarine and agave syrup with a wooden spoon until light and fluffy. Whisk the eggs in a separate bowl. Beat the eggs into the creamed mix a little at a time along with a tablespoon of the flour to stop it from curdling. Sift the flour, baking powder, pinch of salt and cocoa powder and fold it into the egg mixture until well combined. Fold in the milk; this will make the batter looser. Pour onto the prepared baking tin. Smooth out evenly. Bake in the centre of the preheated oven for 20–25 minutes until the centre is firm and spongy to the touch. Place on a wire rack to cool. After 5 minutes, slide the cake from the tin and cool thoroughly on the cooling rack.

3 While the cake base cools, place the cream in a small pot and warm over a medium heat, but do not boil. Break the chocolate into pieces and add to the pot. Lower the heat, stirring gently until it melts completely and the mixture is smooth. Pour the chocolate cream over the cake and smooth out with a knife, allowing it to go over the edges of the cake. If the chocolate topping becomes too thick to pour just add more cream until the correct consistency is reached.

TIP: To make 12 chocolate buns, divide the ingredients in half and follow the method as above, but using a shallow muffin tray. You can use paper cases if you wish but it's not necessary.

TIP: To make a round chocolate sponge cake, follow the recipe and instead of a Swiss roll tin, use two 20 cm Victoria sponge tins. Oil and line the tins with greaseproof paper. When the cakes have cooled, sandwich together with whipped cream. For the topping, use 100 g 70% dark chocolate and 3 tbsp fresh cream and follow the method as above.

TIP: Cream can be omitted from the topping and replaced with 40 g sunflower margarine. Place the chocolate and sunflower margarine into a metal or glass bowl and place over a pot of lightly boiling water. Stir occasionally. When the chocolate has melted and the mixture is smooth, pour over the cooled chocolate cake. It won't be as rich, but it still works well.

TIP: Wholemeal spelt flour can also be used for this cake.

APPLE CAKE WITH CINNAMON

Apple and cinnamon is a classic combination, and this light, flavoursome sponge makes for a moreish, warming cake.

SERVES 12
4 APPLES
30 ML LEMON JUICE
4 FREE RANGE EGGS
150 G SUNFLOWER MARGARINE
250 G AGAVE SYRUP (PLUS EXTRA TO BRUSH THE CAKE)

250 G SET NATURAL YOGHURT
300 G WHOLEMEAL SPELT FLOUR
2¹/₂ TSP BAKING POWDER
1¹/₂ TSP CINNAMON (PLUS EXTRA FOR DUSTING THE CAKE)

1 Peel, quarter and remove the core of the apples. Slice the apples thinly and toss in the lemon juice. This will prevent the apples from going brown. Set aside.

2 Preheat oven to Gas 3/170°C/325°F.

3 Oil and line a 30 x 25 cm baking tin with greaseproof paper. Lightly oil the greaseproof paper.

4 In a large bowl whisk the eggs until fluffy. Add the margarine and whisk. Add the agave syrup and yoghurt and whisk.

5 In a separate bowl, mix the flour, baking powder and cinnamon together. Sieve the dry ingredients into the egg and yoghurt mixture and mix thoroughly with a metal spoon. (I find that mixing a cake with a metal spoon is more thorough at taking it from the sides of the bowl than a wooden spoon. The bowl of the spoon is also deeper, so there's less heavy beating.)

6 Pour onto the prepared baking tray. Layer the apple slices down the centre of the cake mixture, in 3 lines. Bake for 50 minutes until brown and risen. Check the centre with a skewer to make sure it is baked thoroughly. Cool on a baking tray. Brush with agave syrup and a sprinkling of cinnamon when cool.

TIP: When blackberry season comes, try replacing 2 of the apples with 200 g of blackberries. Peel and dice the remaining 2 apples and arrange them with the blackberries on top of the cake mixture. Bake as above.

BANANA AND BLUEBERRY MUFFINS

These are so good with blueberries that we don't even eat the original banana and walnut muffins anymore.

MAKES 12
3 FREE RANGE EGGS
175 G SUNFLOWER MARGARINE
100 G HONEY
100 G AGAVE SYRUP
3 BANANAS
250 G WHOLEMEAL SPELT FLOUR
2 TSP BAKING POWDER
1 HANDFUL BLUEBERRIES, FRESH OR FROZEN

1 Preheat oven to Gas 4/180°C/350°F. Oil and line a 12-cup muffin tray with paper cases. Lightly oil the paper cases. In a large mixing bowl, whisk the eggs for a minute. Add the margarine and whisk until light and fluffy. Add the honey and agave syrup and whisk. Peel and mash the bananas and add to the bowl. Add the flour, baking powder and blueberries to the bowl and mix well. Spoon the muffin mix evenly into the muffin cups. Place in the centre of the preheated oven and bake for 45 minutes until the muffins have risen and are springy to the touch.

2 Top with one of the toppings on p. 175.

CRUMB TOPPING

55 G WHITE SPELT FLOUR
2 TBSP AGAVE SYRUP, MAPLE SYRUP OR CLEAR HONEY
½ TSP CINNAMON
1 TBSP OF SUNFLOWER MARGARINE, MELTED

Place all the ingredients in a bowl and with a fork mix together until a crumb mixture develops. When you spoon the batter into the muffin cups sprinkle the crumb topping on top and place in the centre of a preheated oven and bake for 40–45 minutes.

CHOCOLATE DRIZZLE

60 G 70% DARK CHOCOLATE
1 TBSP SUNFLOWER MARGARINE

Place the chocolate and margarine into a bowl and place over a pot of simmering water until the mix has melted completely. Remove from the heat and drizzle across the cooled baked muffins.

CREAM CHEESE ICING

175 G CREAM CHEESE
1 TBSP THICK NATURAL YOGHURT
2 TBSP MAPLE SYRUP, AGAVE SYRUP OR CLEAR HONEY
½ TSP VANILLA ESSENCE

Place all the ingredients into a bowl and mix well until creamy. When the muffins are baked and cooled, spread the icing on top.

CHOCOLATE BEETROOT CAKE
WITH RICOTTA AND ORANGE

Putting beetroot into a chocolate cake might seem strange but, like apple or carrot, it keeps the cake moist and gives a rich flavour. Worth trying!

SERVES 12
175 G WHOLEMEAL SPELT FLOUR OR FINE WHOLEMEAL FLOUR
55 G COCOA POWDER
1½ TSP BAKING POWDER
SEA SALT
300 G COOKED FRESH BEETROOT
3 FREE RANGE EGGS
150 G SUNFLOWER MARGARINE
200 G AGAVE OR MAPLE SYRUP, OR HONEY
1 TSP VANILLA EXTRACT

FOR THE TOPPING:
5 TBSP RICOTTA CHEESE
2 TBSP AGAVE OR MAPLE SYRUP
GRATED RIND OF 1 MEDIUM ORANGE

1 Preheat oven to Gas 4/180°C/350°F.

2 Lightly oil a 20 cm round or square cake tin. Oil the tin and dust with flour. Shake off the excess flour.

3 Sift flour, cocoa powder, baking powder and a pinch of salt into a bowl. Peel the cooked beetroot if required and blend in a food processor or with a hand blender. Whisk the eggs, agave syrup, margarine and vanilla extract in a large bowl. Stir into the dry mix until well combined. Spoon into the prepared cake tin and spread out until smooth. Bake in the centre of the oven for 40 minutes. Check with a skewer to see that it's cooked through. Leave in the tin for 5 minutes then turn out onto a cooling tray to cool thoroughly.

4 Mix the Ricotta cheese, agave syrup and orange rind and spread generously over the top of the cooled cake and serve.

TIP: Cream cheese, thick yoghurt or whipped fresh cream can be used instead of the Ricotta for the topping.

HOMEMADE FRUIT MINCE PIES

This mince has a very big fruit taste. The long cooking time releases the fruit sugars from the dried fruit so it doesn't need any added refined sugar.

PASTRY (SEE P. 162)

MAKES 600 G OF MINCE
115 G RAISINS
115 G SULTANAS
100 G CURRANTS
55 G PITTED DATES, CHOPPED
70 G COOKING APPLES, WASHED AND CUT INTO SMALL DICE
ORANGE RIND AND JUICE OF 1/4 ORANGE
MIXED SPICE
CINNAMON
NUTMEG
1 TSP MUGI MISO
1 TBSP WALNUTS, CHOPPED SMALL
1 TBSP APPLE CONCENTRATE

FOR THE ALMOND TOPPING:
125 G GROUND ALMONDS
NATURAL ALMOND ESSENCE

1 Wash the raisins, sultanas, currants and dates. Place in a heavy-bottomed pot along with the chopped apple, orange rind and juice and the mixed spice, cinnamon and nutmeg. Mix well. Add water to just cover the fruit. Bring to a boil, lower the heat, cover tightly and simmer for 1 hour. Stir occasionally. When the cooking is finished, stir in the walnuts, apple concentrate and miso. Set aside to cool.

2 The miso acts as a preservative, so the fruit mince will keep for 3 months in the fridge.

3 This amount of fruit will make 12 mince pies with almond topping using the wholemeal pastry recipe on p. 162.

4 Preheat oven to Gas 5/190°C/375°F.

5 Lightly oil a 12-cup muffin tray. Roll out the pastry on a lightly floured surface to 1/4 cm thickness. Using a 9 cm scone cutter, cut out 12 circles of pastry. Line the muffin tray with the pastry circles. Press them gently into the base of the muffin tray so that the pastry comes   of the way up the muffin cup. Bake for 20 minutes. Once baked, these bases will keep for 2 weeks in an airtight container. They also freeze well.

6 To assemble the pies, place 125 g ground almonds into the bowl of a food processor or use a hand blender. Add a few drops of natural almond essence and 300 ml water and blend until smooth. Set aside.

7 Spoon the fruit mince into the baked pastry cases. Using a dessertspoon, add a layer of almond topping over the mince. Bake for 20–30 minutes or until the topping is lightly golden.

FRUIT MINCE AND PEAR STRUDEL

This dessert is an indulgent alternative to mince pies at Christmastime, and is made lighter by the pears and orange zest.

SERVES 4 TO 5
300 G FRUIT MINCE (P. 179)

70 G SUNFLOWER MARGARINE
115 G BREADCRUMBS
RIND OF ½ AN ORANGE, FINELY GRATED, ABOUT 2 TSP
2 PEARS, RIPE BUT FIRM
5 SHEETS OF FILO PASTRY
EXTRA VIRGIN OLIVE OIL

1 Preheat oven to Gas 4/180°C/350°F.

2 Heat a pan over a medium heat and melt the margarine. Add the breadcrumbs and fry until golden and crunchy, approximately 10 minutes. Add the grated orange rind.

3 Peel the pears, cut into quarters and core. Slice the quarters thinly (¼ cm slices), place in a bowl and add the fruit mince. Mix well.

4 Heat the oven. Oil a baking sheet. Pour some olive oil into a small bowl. Lay the 5 sheets of filo pastry onto a flat surface. Take 1 sheet of pastry and lay onto a flat surface with the longest side closest to you. Brush lightly with the olive oil. Lay another sheet of pastry flat on top of the first. Lightly brush with olive oil and sprinkle with ⅓ of the toasted breadcrumbs. Repeat with two more sheets, oil and breadcrumbs. Lay the last sheet of pastry on top of the prepared pastry.

5 Lay the pear and fruit mince mix down one side of the pastry, stopping 5 cm from the long edge and the ends of the pastry. The mix should cover a strip 5 cm in width. Fold over each end and fold the side closest to you over the fruit mix and begin rolling up the strudel, tucking it in firmly as you roll. Don't worry if the pastry begins to crumble a little or looks uneven, this will add to the look of the strudel when it is baked. Place on the oiled baking sheet and lightly oil the strudel. Bake in the centre of the preheated oven for 20 minutes, until golden.

6 Delicious with yoghurt, crème fraîche or a cashew nut cream. **To make cashew nut cream**, place 2 handfuls of nuts into a blender, or if using a hand blender a deep jug or bowl. Add water and blend. Continue adding water gradually and blending until a smooth, runny cream has formed. This is a lovely vegan cream to serve with any dessert or cake.

FIG AND PEAR ROLL WITH CARDAMOM

Quite simply the mother of all fig rolls, this crunchy treat is a must for anyone who likes to munch on the store-bought variety with their cup of tea.

MAKES 4 TO 8 PIECES
250 G DRIED FIGS
1 PEAR
3 GREEN CARDAMOM PODS
25 G WALNUTS, TOASTED

FOR THE PASTRY:
100 G WHOLEMEAL SPELT FLOUR
75 G WHITE SPELT FLOUR
SEA SALT
85 G SUNFLOWER MARGARINE
2 TSP AGAVE SYRUP

1 To make the pastry, place both the flours in a large bowl and mix in a pinch of salt. Rub in the margarine with the flours until the mix resembles breadcrumbs. Add the agave syrup and 20 ml cold water. Using your hands, bring the mix together until a ball of dough forms. Wrap in cling film and leave to rest for 30 minutes in the fridge.

2 Wash the figs and place in a pot with 350 ml water and bring to a boil. Lower the heat, cover and simmer for 10 minutes. Set aside to cool, reserving the liquid.

3 Preheat oven to Gas 5/190°C/375°F.

4 Peel, quarter and core the pear. Chop into approx. 1 cm pieces. Place into a pot along with 150 ml of water and bring to a boil. Lower the heat, cover and simmer for 10–15 minutes until tender. Set aside to cool.

5 When the figs have cooled, remove the stems, chop the figs and place in a bowl. Crack the cardamom pods to remove the seeds, and stir the seeds into the figs along with the cooked pear. If the mix is stiff, add some of the reserved fig and pear juices or water. Mix well.

6 To assemble the fig roll, first lightly oil a baking tray. Take the dough from the fridge roll out on a floured surface. Roll out until the dough is 1/4 cm in thickness. Cut into a 25 x 15 cm rectangle.

7 Place the rectangle of pastry, with the longest side across, in front of you. Chop the toasted walnuts, sprinkle them over pastry and press down lightly into the dough. Spread the fig, pear and cardamom mix across the pastry, 5 cm from the bottom. The fig and pear strip should be 5 cm thick. Roll up and place on the baking tray seam side down.

8 Place in the preheated oven for 30–40 minutes until lightly golden.

9 This cake keeps very well in an airtight container in the fridge.

GLOSSARY

Some of the ingredients we use in this book might be unfamiliar to you. Here, I have written a little about them to explain what they are and why we use them as part of a wholefood diet. Once upon a time, such ingredients were only available in our deli, health food shops, Asian food stores and some specialist food shops, but now, almost all of them are available in large chain supermarkets on their specialty, gluten-free and 'ethnic' food shelves – just ask!

Though Blazing Salads works with organic ingredients in all our food, I understand that it may not be practical to do so in each and every dish you make. Ultimately, the important thing is that you use the best-quality ingredients you can afford to get the best out of your food for your health and well-being.

ASIAN INGREDIENTS

BROWN RICE VINEGAR

This vinegar is made from water and brown rice that has been aged for several months. It has a full-bodied but subtly sweet taste. Great sprinkled on sliced fresh beetroot or sliced avocado.

KUZU

Kuzu is the powdered tuber from the root of the hardy wild kuzu plant. It is a very good thickening agent. It also soothes the stomach and the intestines and helps to strengthen them.

MISO

Miso is a paste made from soya beans, salt and grain and fermented with a special enzyme called koji. It is fermented for 6 months to 2 years. I like mugi (barley) miso best for everyday cooking. Unpasteurised miso offers the best nutritional value and is a 'live' food.

Anyone eating a vegetarian or vegan diet would benefit from eating miso every day as it is rich in protein, easily digestible and contains vitamin B12.

Miso soup is a nice, simple way of using miso, and if it includes dulse or wakame seaweed, will add extra iron and calcium to your diet.

SEAWEEDS

Seaweeds are an excellent addition to your diet as they have a high mineral content and can help lower cholesterol and fat in the body. They help to cleanse the blood and strengthen the liver. Seaweeds have a high amount of calcium, iodine and iron.

Some seaweeds, like dulse or dillisk, are harvested in Ireland, and are high in iodine and iron.

KOMBU is another member of the kelp family. It helps to carry toxic and radioactive waste from the body and promotes hair growth and a clear complexion. Used in the cooking of beans, it helps to soften them and to make them more digestible.

WAKAME is one of the seaweeds highest in calcium. It is a lovely light green colour. Use in miso soup, soups and stews and salads.

ARAME is not harvested in Ireland but is worth including in your diet as it has a particularly mild flavour that most will find palatable. Black and stringy, it has the highest amount of calcium of any seaweed.

NORI is called 'sloke' in Ireland and 'laver' in Wales, and is native the Irish Sea. It is best known as norimaki for sushi rolls. It is the highest in protein of all the seaweeds, rich in vitamin A, B1 and niacin. It is a diuretic and aids the digestion. It is very easy to prepare, as it comes dried in sheets. Hold a sheet over a naked flame to toast for a few minutes. Crumble over grains, salad or soup.

SOYA SAUCE

Good quality soya sauce does not contain monosodium glutamate, caramel, sugar or refined salt, provides extra nutrition and is rich in protein. Soya sauce is made from soya beans, water and sea salt and allowed age for anywhere from a few months to a year. There are two main varieties, tamari and shoyu. Tamari is full-bodied and wheat-free. Shoyu is a little lighter as it contains wheat berries. Kikkoman, a popular brand of soy sauce, is full-bodied also and wheat-free.

TAHINI

Tahini is a paste made by grinding hulled sesame seeds. It is an ingredient in hummus and can be used to add a rich flavour to bean and vegetable stews. It contains all the nutritional value of sesame seeds.

TOFU

Tofu is a curd made from soya beans, which, though a source of good quality protein, are difficult to digest in their natural state. To make them more digestible, the beans are soaked, blended, and cooked. The soya purée is then mixed with calcium sulphate to set it. The whey is then poured off and the curd cut into small blocks – tofu. As it is made from soy beans, tofu contains B vitamins, minerals, calcium, iron, sodium and potassium, and is low in fat.

To store, keep covered with water in a container in the fridge. Change the water daily and it should keep for a week.

BEANS

Beans are a very good source of protein. They are rich in calcium, iron, potassium and B vitamins and low in fat. When beans are combined with a grain, they make a complete protein. People often think that you need to eat large amounts of beans in order to get enough protein, but that's not true! Two tablespoons of beans at a meal is enough . Young children may find it hard to digest beans, so it is important to cook them properly. Wait until a child is over 18 months before introducing beans or lentils to their diet.

Soak beans overnight or for 6–8 hours in plenty of cold water. Pour off the soaking liquid and cover with 2 cm of fresh water. Do not use salt during the cooking as it prevents the beans from softening. I recommend adding a small piece of rinsed kombu seaweed to the pot. Kombu seaweed will add extra nutrition, promote faster cooking and help to make them more digestible. Most beans will take 40 minutes cooking after soaking, but chickpeas take an hour.

GRAINS

Grains are beneficial towards maintaining a balanced vegetarian diet or wholefood diet. The grains should be of the highest quality.

When rinsing grains, lentils, beans, dried fruit, place in a bowl and rinse in plenty of cold water. Husks and dirt particles are light, so they will float to the top and can be poured off. Repeat about 3 times. Do not use a sieve as all the larger particles of dirt just fall to the bottom of the sieve and are emptied into your food.

BARLEY

Barley is another of the oldest cultivated grains. It has a chewy texture, is easy to digest and is very nourishing. It is lovely served in soups, stews and salads. It is best to use hulled barley as it still has its vitamin-rich outer layers.

BUCKWHEAT

Buckwheat is a great winter grain; it contains the bioflavinoid rutin, a supplement used in the treatment of bad blood circulation, so it's very warming. It also helps to reduce high blood pressure.

BULGUR

Bulgur wheat is high in fibre, rich in B vitamins, iron, calcium and phosphorus. It is a low GI food. Bulgur is made from wheat berries that are boiled, then dried and cracked. It is very quick to cook, and has a nutty flavour and coarse texture.

BROWN RICE

Brown rice is high in B vitamins and is beneficial to the nervous system. 100% whole brown rice has all the vitamins, minerals, amino acids, and proteins that the body needs for a balanced diet.

MILLET

Millet is the only alkaline grain so it's perfect for those who suffer from an excess of acid. High in protein, iron and B vitamins, it is a diuretic and strengthens the kidneys. It is one of the oldest cultivated grains in the world. Millet cooks relatively quickly, taking 30 minutes.

OATS

Oats help to lower cholesterol and strengthen the cardiac muscles. Oats contain B vitamins, iron and potassium. They are a low GI food, which means that they can help to control blood glucose levels by maintaining blood glucose levels after a meal and providing a steady release of energy.

QUINOA

Quinoa (pronounced keen-wa) is not a grain, but can be used as one. It is light and quick and easy to prepare. It is a great for vegetarians because it is very high in protein, calcium and is a good source of iron, B vitamins and vitamin E. Quinoa is also gluten-free.

FLOURS

BROWN RICE FLOUR

Brown rice flour is gluten-free. Brown rice flour is recommended because it has more vitamins and minerals than white rice flour. It is a perfect thickener for soups and stews; just shake straight into the soup or stew at the end of cooking and stir. It will not go lumpy!

SPELT FLOUR

We use spelt flour in the Blazing Salads deli because our customers find it easier to digest and I have found that the wholemeal spelt flour makes lovely pastry with a nutty flavour. It is lovely and light and suits our cake baking.

Spelt is an ancient grain. It is high in protein and is a good source of calcium, selenium, zinc, iron, and manganese. It contains B vitamins, especially niacin and vitamin A, and amino acids.

Throughout this book, spelt flour can be replaced with white or wholemeal wheat flour.

SEEDS

Pumpkin, sunflower and sesame seeds are high-energy foods. They are high in protein, phosphorus, magnesium, iron, vitamins A, E, F and the B vitamins niacin and riboflavin.

Pumpkin seeds are a valuable source of zinc and omega-3 fatty acids. Pumpkin oil is made from pumpkin seeds to use as a dressing for salad, and as a seed spread.

SUNFLOWER seeds are the highest in iron of these three seeds, and as a bonus, they also contain a good amount of copper, which helps assimilate iron, in addition to all the 10 amino acids. Sunflower oil, extracted from the seeds, can be used in cooking, in salad dressing, and as a seed spread.

SESAME SEEDS are rich in both calcium and copper, and are made into an oil for use in cooking and in salad dressing, and as a paste, tahini (see above).

GOMASIO, or **SESAME SALT**, is a condiment that has a lovely nutty aroma and taste. Using salt mixes like gomasio helps you to reduce the amount of salt you add to your food, plus all the benefits of sesame seeds – calcium, magnesium, iron, protein and fibre. To make, toast the sesame seeds on a dry pan until the seeds can be crumbled easily between your fingers, about 15 minutes. Place 10 parts sesame seeds and 1 part sea salt in a mortar and pestle and grind until about eighty per cent of the seeds are powdered. If you have children, this is a job they will enjoy – it was one of my first jobs in my parents' restaurant. If the gomasio is for children, use 20 parts sesame seeds to 1 part sea salt. Keep in an airtight container. It is best made fresh weekly.

SWEETENERS

AGAVE SYRUP

Agave syrup is extracted from the agave plant, which is a member of the cactus family. Unlike sugar, it has a low GI index rating, so it will not alter your blood sugar levels dramatically, and unlike some sugars, it is vegan. We sweeten our cakes with it as it has a light taste that doesn't overpower, and has a good level of sweetness. Maple syrup is a good substitute for agave.

APPLE CONCENTRATE (NO ADDED SUGAR VARIETY)

A great sweetener to have in your cupboard, apple concentrate is low GI. Use to sweeten stewed fruit, salad dressings, cookies and some baked products. If using as a drink, dilute 1 part apple concentrate and 10 parts water, or more water if it's for very young children.

BROWN RICE SYRUP

A lovely, mild sweetener that is also low GI. Use to sweeten stewed fruits or cookies. Also nice instead of honey in salad dressings.

MAPLE SYRUP

100% Maple syrup is a natural sweetener with an excellent oaky flavour. Great with pancakes, and as a substitute to sugar in baking. Adds a wonderful flavour to bakewell tart and keeps it nice and moist.

FATS

SUNFLOWER MARGARINE

We use sunflower margarine in our baking at Blazing Salads as it is dairy-free, and we have found that it works well in cake-baking and pastry-making.

When choosing a margarine, check the nutritional facts on the label. Look for one with low trans-fatty acids and one that is low in saturated fat. Some margarines can even help to lower cholesterol.

The sunflower margarine in these recipes can be replaced with an equal amount of butter.

UNREFINED OILS

Using a variety of unrefined oils in your cooking is a simple way to give yourself and your family the nutritional benefit of extra vitamins and minerals. In unrefined oils, the majority of vitamins and minerals found in the seed or nut remain in the oil (provided it isn't overheated) and have a very high content of unsaturated fatty acids.

There is a great variety of unrefined oils available; sesame, sunflower, olive and rapeseed are good for cooking and dressings alike, and pumpkin, hazelnut and walnut oils are best in dressings for cold dishes and salads.

Unrefined oils are not suitable for deep-frying, as they are too rich and heavy and burn easily at high temperatures. Instead, use a standard vegetable, sunflower, soya or peanut oil.

MEASUREMENT CHARTS

METRIC	IMPERIAL	METRIC	IMPERIAL
5 g	⅛ oz	325 g	11½ oz
10 g	¼ oz	350 g	12 oz
15 g	½ oz	375 g	13 oz
20 g	¾ oz	400 g	14 oz
25 g	1 oz	425 g	15 oz
35 g	1¼ oz	450 g	1 lb
40 g	1½ oz	500 g	1 lb 2 oz
50 g	1¾ oz	550 g	1 lb 4 oz
55 g	2 oz	600 g	1 lb 5 oz
60 g	2¼ oz	650 g	1 lb 7 oz
70 g	2½ oz	700 g	1 lb 9 oz
75 g	2¾ oz	750 g	1 lb 10 oz
85 g	3 oz	800 g	1 lb 12 oz
90 g	3¼ oz	850 g	1 lb 14 oz
100 g	3½ oz	900 g	2 lb
115 g	4 oz	950 g	2 lb 2 oz
125 g	4½ oz	1 kg	2 lb 4 oz
140 g	5 oz	1.25 kg	2 lb 12 oz
150 g	5½ oz	1.3 kg	3 lb
175 g	6 oz	1.5 kg	3 lb 5 oz
200 g	7 oz	1.6 kg	3 lb 8 oz
225 g	8 oz	1.8 kg	4 lb
250 g	9 oz	2 kg	4 lb 8 oz
275 g	9¾ oz	2.25 kg	5 lb
280 g	10 oz	2.5 kg	5 lb 8 oz
300 g	10½ oz	2.7 kg	6 lb
315 g	11 oz	3 kg	6 lb 8 oz

OVEN TEMPERATURES

CELCIUS	FAHRENHEIT	GAS
110°C	225°F	¼
120°C	250°F	½
140°C	275°F	1
150°C	300°F	2
160°C	325°F	3
170°C	325°F	3
180°C	350°F	4
190°C	375°F	5
200°C	400°F	6
220°C	425°F	7
230°C	450°F	8

SPOONS

METRIC	IMPERIAL
1.25 ml	¼ tsp
2.5 ml	½ tsp
5 ml	1 tsp
10 ml	2 tsp
15 ml	3 tsp / 1 tbsp
30 ml	2 tbsp
45 ml	3 tbsp
60 ml	4 tbsp
75 ml	5 tbsp
90 ml	6 tbsp

US CUPS

CUPS	METRIC
¼ cup	60 ml
⅓ cup	70 ml
½ cup	125 ml
⅔ cup	150 ml
¾ cup	175 ml
1 cup	250 ml
1½ cups	375 ml
2 cups	500 ml
3 cups	750 ml
4 cups	1 litre

VOLUME

METRIC	IMPERIAL	METRIC	IMPERIAL	METRIC	IMPERIAL
25 ml	1 fl oz	300 ml	10 fl oz	1 litre	1¼ pints
50 ml	2 fl oz	350 ml	12 fl oz	1.2 litres	2 pints
75 ml	2½ fl oz	400 ml	14 fl oz	1.3 litres	2¼ pints
100 ml	3½ fl oz	425 ml	15 fl oz	1.4 litres	2½ pints
125 ml	4 fl oz	450 ml	16 fl oz	1.5 litres	2¾ pints
150 ml	5 fl oz	500 ml	18 fl oz	1.7 litres	3 pints
175 ml	6 fl oz	568 ml	20 fl oz	2 litres	3½ pints
200 ml	7 fl oz	600 ml	1 pint	2.5 litres	4½ pints
225 ml	8 fl oz	700 ml	1¼ pints	2.8 litres	5 pints
250 ml	9 fl oz	850 ml	1½ pints	3 litres	5¼ pints

INDEX

Page numbers set in **_bold italic_** indicate photographs.